J. R. R. Tolkien

J. R. R. Tolkien

CREATOR OF LANGUAGES AND LEGENDS

DORIS LYNCH

FRANKLIN WATTS
A Division of Scholastic Inc.
New York Toronto London Auckland Sydney
Mexico City New Delhi Hong Kong
Danbury, Connecticut

For Thom, Kris, and Cody Jack

ACKNOWLEDGEMENTS

I am grateful to the staffs of The Tolkien Archives at Marquette University, Milwaukee, Wisconsin, and The Marion E. Wade Center at Wheaton College, Wheaton, Illinois. Thanks to my writing group for encouragement.

Photographs © 2003: Birmingham Library Services: 35; Birmingham Picture Library/Jonathan Berg: 17, 24, 66; Bridgeman Art Library International Ltd., London/New York: 20 (Chris Beetles Ltd., London, UK), 73 (Mayor Gallery, London, UK), 56 (Private Collection); Christie's Images Ltd.: 92, 100, 102; Corbis Images: 2 (Bettmann), 46 (Chris Andrews Publications), 13, 48 (Hulton-Deutsch Collection); Getty Images: 91 (London Daily Express), 108; Governors of King Edward the Sixth Schools in Birmingham: 26, 29, 40; Hulton | Archive/Getty Images: cover, 22, 61, 76, 89, 101, 110; Used by permission of Marion E. Wade Center, Wheaton College, Wheaton, IL: 88 (photograph by Stephen W. Mead), 86; Mary Evans Picture Library: 18; Photofest: 84, 97 top, 97 center, 97 bottom, 104; Reprinted by permission of Oxford University Press: 68 (from *The OUP: An Informal History*, by Peter Sutcliffe, 1978).

The quotation from the Oral History Interview with C. L. Wiseman is used with the permission of the copyright owner, The Marion E. Wade Center, Wheaton College, Wheaton, Illinois, © 1987 (and may not be further reproduced without written consent).

Library of Congress Cataloging-in-Publication Data
Lynch, Doris
J. R. R. Tolkien: creator of languages and legends / by Doris Lynch
   p. cm. — (Great life stories)
Includes bibliographical references and index.
Contents: An ocean voyage—A home in Hobbitland—Animalic, Nevbosh, and Naffarin—Tea clubs and poetry—From hospital elves to forest muses—Walrus to Leeds—Oxford again—On hobbits and fairy stories—Beyond hobbits—Lightning from a clear sky—The Shire lives on.
ISBN 0-531-12253-0 (lib. bdg.)
1. Tolkien, J. R. R. (John Ronald Reuel), 1892–1973—Juvenile literature. 2. Fantasy fiction, English—History and criticism—Juvenile literature. 3. Authors, English—20th century—Biography—Juvenile literature. 4. Imaginary languages in literature—Juvenile literature. 5. Middle Earth (Imaginary place)—Juvenile literature. I. Title. II. Series.
PR6039.O32Z693 2003
828'.91209—dc21
[B]
2003000958

Contents

Introduction

"In a hole in the ground there lived a hobbit." With these words, John Ronald Reuel Tolkien began *The Hobbit,* one of the best-loved children's books of all time. Hobbits are creatures that are about 3 feet (1 meter) tall. Their round bellies show their love of food. They can't grow beards, but they do grow thick, curly hair on their toes. Best of all, they don't ever need to wear shoes—because their feet grow thick soles.

Shortly before this century began, readers in Great Britain were polled. What did they consider the best book of the twentieth century? They chose *The Lord of the Rings.* Many critics consider this trilogy—a series of three related books that continue the same story—to be Tolkien's masterpiece. A similar poll in the United States also rated the trilogy in the top hundred.

Tolkien's novels belong to a category of fiction known as fantasy writing. In fantasies, authors describe other worlds or imagine this world at other times. Fantasy differs from science fiction. In science fiction, the story being told might someday happen. But what occurs in fantasy novels will never happen. Tolkien inspired a whole new generation of fantasy writers by proving that this category of books could be very popular.

The Hobbit and *The Lord of the Rings* were more than works of fantasy. In addition to being a great storyteller, Tolkien constructed an entirely new world. He named this world Middle-earth.

Middle-earth was similar to northern Europe but set in the distant past. To complete his novels, Tolkien had to imagine this world fully. He drew maps of Middle-earth. His son, Christopher, also helped with this cartography, or mapmaking. Tolkien also made up hundreds of place names. Some of these include the Shire, Encircling Mountains, Deeping Coomb, Laurelindórenan, and the Caverns of Helm's Deep.

Not only did Tolkien provide his imaginary world with physical details, but he also gave it legendary ones. He developed myths and stories of past heroes. However, what Tolkien loved to do most was to invent languages. Tolkien gave many of his imaginary creatures their own languages. As Professor Jane Chance wrote in *The Lord of the Rings: The Mythology of Power*, Tolkien "knew that words were magic." Many times he insisted that it was this process of language invention that inspired him to become a writer. He wrote novels in order to have a place to display his languages.

The Hobbit and *The Lord of the Rings* remain Tolkien's most famous works, but he also wrote many other books. Some of these include *The Silmarillion*, *Mr. Bliss*, *Roverandom*, *The Monsters and the Critics*, and *Farmer Giles of Ham*. People all over the world recognize Tolkien's name easily. In the article "Elvish Lives," Jon Fishman, drummer for the band Phish, spoke of Tolkien's influence on our culture. "Tolkien is part of the molecules you breathe in your artistic surroundings, whether or not you've actually ever read Tolkien."

Tolkien's fame did not rest solely on his being a popular writer. He also received honors for being a great teacher and a researcher of the

English language. As a professor, Tolkien researched the literature and languages of early Britain. He also taught many languages, including Icelandic, Finnish, Old English, and Middle English. Tolkien also shared with his students many important works from the Middle Ages.

Not many grown men think about dragons, but Tolkien did. In a Christmas lecture in 1937, the year *The Hobbit* came out, he spoke to an audience of children about dragons. He described dragons as being of two kinds: "creeping and winged." That day, Tolkien also showed the children drawings he had made of dragons. Tolkien's fascination with dragons began when he was very young. His mother read him fairy tales about the gigantic beasts. Tolkien became so curious about dragons that he learned to read at a young age to find out more about them.

In the late 1960s, Tolkien injured his right hand. For weeks he could not write. In a letter quoted by Humphrey Carpenter in his introduction to Tolkien's published letters, Tolkien complained about what an immense hardship this caused him. Not being able to use a writing tool was "as defeating as the loss of her beak would be to a hen." Tolkien's pen introduced millions of readers to fantasy creatures who roamed Middle-earth long ago. Without Tolkien's writing, the world would be empty of hobbits and a much poorer place.

ONE

An Ocean Voyage

On January 3, 1892, Mabel Tolkien gave birth to her first child. Mabel and her husband, Arthur, named the infant "John" after Arthur's maternal grandfather. They gave the baby two middle names: Ronald and Reuel. At first, they could not agree which name to call their son. Arthur preferred John Reuel; Mabel favored Ronald. In the end, Mabel won.

Arthur Tolkien had shipped off to South Africa in the late 1880s. He left England in search of a better livelihood. Lloyds Bank of Birmingham, where he worked, offered him security, but Arthur needed a higher salary. He wanted to marry his sweetheart, Mabel Suffield. As a dutiful eldest son, Arthur had stayed home to care for his younger brothers and sisters. Now that they had grown up, he was free to start his own family.

In the 1870s and 1880s, explorers discovered major deposits of gold and diamonds in South Africa. Business boomed. Thousands of miners rushed to the African continent. Many stayed. They became ranchers, farmers, and storekeepers. Many needed bankers to handle their finances.

For Arthur, the African gamble paid off. He worked at various bank branches from Cape Town to Johannesburg. Because he worked hard, his supervisors offered him a position as manager of a branch of the Bank of South Africa. This bank was located in Bloemfontein, the capital of the Orange Free State, an independent region in southern Africa. It lay about 625 miles (1,000 kilometers) from Cape Town.

With some reservations, Mabel's father consented to her marriage to the thirty-four-year-old banker. Mabel boarded the steamship *Roslin Castle* in March of 1891. She had just turned twenty-one. On April 16, 1891, Arthur and Mabel were married in the cathedral of Cape Town. After a brief honeymoon, the couple journeyed mostly by rail to Bloemfontein.

One Land, Many Claims

In the 1830s, many Afrikaners (descendents of European settlers) left the Cape Colony in South Africa to escape British rule. Thousands of settlers marched northward. Their journey became known as *The Great Trek*. The Afrikaners forced the native peoples off the lands they settled. They carved farms out of the countryside. The British fought the settlers over this area, but lost. In 1854, the Afrikaners named their new territory the Orange Free State, because it was bounded by the Orange River.

Bloemfontein received its name from a fountain on the west side of town. Johannes Nicolaas Brits, an early Dutch settler, discovered this spring on his property. As recalled by W. W. Collins in an early history of Bloemfontein, Brits named his farm, which later became the town site, *bloem der fontein*. In Dutch, these words mean "flower fountain."

The hot frontier town did not impress Mabel. Fierce winds blew off the veldt, or African grassland. Outside of town, springboks, wildebeests, and the occasional leopard roamed. At night jackals prowled the plains that surrounded town. Occasionally, the newlyweds heard an animal roar in the darkness. "Owlin Wilderness! Horrid Waste!" Mabel wrote to her family in Birmingham, according to Tolkien's biographer, Humphrey Carpenter. These words summarized her low opinion of her new home.

The bank manager's house on Maitland Street had a balcony. Arthur worked at the bank next door. Although Bloemfontein boasted a tennis club, a parliament house, a small garrison (military encampment), a library,

Bloemfontein was founded in 1846. Today the city plays a major role in the South African government because the Supreme Court of Appeal meets there.

a hospital, and a club for residents from Europe, it still resembled a frontier town much more than the capital of a territory. Dust storms blasted through town. Trees planted by the settlers wilted and died. Mabel began to count the months until the family could travel back to England on home leave.

Arthur loved Africa. The wilderness appealed to him. He even enjoyed the harsh climate. Extremely hot summers gave way to bitter, wind-swept winters. Mabel continued to long for England, but their scheduled leave remained months away. However, two events occurred that moved up their planned visit to England. Mabel gave birth to a second son, Hilary, in February of 1894. Then Ronald became ill. Mabel and Arthur decided that she should travel to England with the boys. Arthur would join them as soon as he could.

FIRST RECOLLECTIONS

All his life Ronald retained vivid memories of Africa. He recalled a particularly strong memory in an interview with journalist Philip Norman. "I was nearly bitten by a snake and I was stung by a tarantula . . . in my garden. All I can remember is a very hot day, long, dead grass and running. I don't even remember screaming."

Another scary memory that Ronald shared with Norman recalled an event that occurred when he was very young. In those days, Bloemfontein's European families hired native household help. Isaac, who worked for the Tolkiens, spirited the young toddler away. He brought Ronald to his *kraal*, or native village. He kept Ronald there for several days. Although this event worried Ronald's parents very much, in some ways young Ronald enjoyed the adventure. Tolkien told Philip Norman one amusing outcome of the incident. Isaac later named his newborn son Isaac Mister Tolkien Victor "Isaac after himself, Mister Tolkien after my father and Victor—ha! ha!—after Queen Victoria." Queen Victoria ruled England at the time.

Ronald held one special memory of Africa close to his heart. For years afterward, he could shut his eyes and see his father crouched on the floor. His father dipped a brush into a can of paint. Then he slapped his name, A. R. Tolkien, on the family trunk.

FIRST LOSSES

Mabel and the children sailed to England in April of 1895. They went to Birmingham, to a neighborhood called King's Heath. There, in the geographic center of England, Mabel's family lived.

In Birmingham, Ronald enjoyed hearing stories of his family's past. He enjoyed meeting all his relatives: cousins, aunts, uncles, and grandparents. He loved discovering new books of fairy tales. But he missed his father. The following autumn, the family received bitter news from South Africa. Arthur had contracted rheumatic fever. Related to strep throat, this disease seldom strikes adults. Children usually suffer from it. In those days, many people died from it. Arthur felt pain in his joints and his heart became swollen. Today doctors can prescribe antibiotics to treat this disease. However, in the 1890s, these drugs had not been discovered.

Because of Arthur's illness, Mabel bought tickets on a ship bound for South Africa. She planned to return to Bloemfontein with her two boys. She needed to care for their sick father. However, in February, the family received a telegram. Arthur had suffered a severe hemorrhage, which is a massive outpouring of blood. This occurs either inside or outside the body.

Arthur died on February 15, 1896, from complications of rheumatic fever. The banker's friends buried Arthur in the Anglican graveyard in Bloemfontein. Ronald never saw his father again, nor the country of his birth. In one stroke of fate, he suffered two great losses: the death of his beloved father, and the loss of his first home.

However, there were consolations. Ronald spent many days visiting both his mother's and father's relatives in Birmingham. His mother introduced him to places his father had loved: parks, busy downtown New Street, his father's grammar school. At night, the family gathered around the piano. Ronald enjoyed listening to his relatives and their lodgers (paying guests) play popular songs.

Near the end of his life, Denis Gerrolt interviewed the author on BBC Radio. Ronald explained what a great advantage it had been to live in two vastly different places as a child. Moving from South Africa to England as a young child, had made it possible for him to retain vivid memories of his birthplace. Other people can't remember their childhoods, Tolkien said in that 1970 interview, because "it's like constantly photographing the same thing on the same plate. Slight changes simply make a blur. But if a child had a sudden break like that, it's conscious. . . ." Even though he left Africa when he was very young, Ronald remembered the country of his birth very clearly. What's more, when he came to England, he saw the landscape of his ancestors with fresh eyes.

TWO

A Home in Hobbitland

All his life, Ronald felt a deep love for the Warwickshire countryside. Mabel settled there in the tiny community of Sarehole with her two sons. Sarehole consisted of little more than a row of cottages and a mill.

From this cottage, the Tolkien's Sarehole home, Ronald and his brother explored the surrounding country-side of woods, villages, bogs, and streams. Ronald later translated the area surrounding it into the beautiful "Shire" of his novels.

Because no poisonous snakes slithered through the grass, Mabel let her boys roam free. They explored Hall Green, which was the closest village. There in the countryside, Ronald first learned to appreciate nature. In the summer meadows, wild thistles, tansies, and ox-eye daisies grew. Swans swam in the millpond. Brilliant dragonflies dodged each other over dark pools. Water from the Big Mill cascaded down, foamy and wild. Downstream, the boys scooped for minnows that darted back and forth near the banks of the stream.

Willow trees bordered Coldbath Brook. Ronald's love for trees dates from his Sarehole days. In an interview with Denis and Charlotte Plimmer years later, Ronald recalled Sarehole. "It was a very tree-ish part, like open parkland." Ronald recalled the majestic willow, which he taught himself to climb. It spread its graceful fronds over the millpond. One day, as he and his brother raced past, they discovered that their favorite tree had been chopped down. Ronald felt a great sense of loss.

When Ronald was five years old, Queen Victoria celebrated the sixtieth anniversary of her coronation. Besides reigning as monarch of England and Ireland, Queen Victoria also was Empress of India from 1876 until her death in 1901.

Fashion by Fauntelroy

In the late 1880s, a fashion craze spread across the Atlantic. It even reached rural Sarehole. Francis Hodgson Burnett wrote a novel called *Little Lord Fauntelroy* in 1886. The suit worn by the title character inspired a buying frenzy among mothers. The Little Lord Fauntelroy suit consisted of velvet knee-length pants, a fancy shirt, and a broad sash. An accompanying jacket sported a lace collar. Mothers loved this frilly suit, while most boys hated it with passion.

During the time the Tolkien family lived in Sarehole, England honored Queen Victoria's Diamond Jubilee. All across England, people celebrated the sixtieth anniversary of the queen's coronation. Ronald remembered hurrying up the hill toward Moseley Grammar School. The school looked dazzling. Teachers had strung up hundreds of colored lights for the queen's anniversary.

Mabel let Ronald's and Hilary's hair grow long, much longer than the fashion of the 1890s. Children teased the boys because of their girlish hair and their fancy velvet suits. They called the brothers "wenches." Later, when Ronald grew interested in language, he remembered how the Sarehole children had used this old-fashioned word. Since about 1300, the word "wenche" (or "wench") has meant a country girl or young woman.

At both Sarehole and Birmingham at his grandparents' house, Ronald heard words that he had never heard spoken when they lived in South Africa. In particular, Sarehole's country words and local names fascinated the young boy. Already, Ronald's attention had begun to focus on words and their meaning.

This illustration is from a book by George MacDonald, one of Tolkien's favorite authors. Both writers shared an intense love for the English countryside.

FIRST LESSONS

At Sarehole, Mabel began to teach the boys. When she was young, Mabel had learned French, Latin, and German. Because students in England at that time studied several languages in elementary school, Mabel began to teach her sons the Latin and German alphabets and the basic vocabularies of those languages. She also introduced Ronald to the history of words. This subject is known as etymology. Mabel quickly saw that her eldest son showed a strong interest in learning all he could about words.

Mabel also loved fairy tales and myths. At night, she read fairy tales written by the Brothers Grimm as well as English fairy tales, which she remembered from her own childhood. Ronald became fascinated by the underground-dwelling goblins featured in George MacDonald's books.

Mabel also provided the boys with paper and drawing pencils. She encouraged Ronald to draw. She also tried to interest him in music, which was one of her passions. Although Hilary enjoyed music, Ronald clung stubbornly to books and art.

Because they relied on relatives to pay their living expense, Mabel decided that Ronald should secure a scholarship for his schooling. Only then could he get the best education possible. Unfortunately, Ronald had begun to play with words, inventing new ones for his amusement. He did this instead of studying Latin or French. Although Mabel recognized Ronald's great verbal abilities, she discouraged his attempts at inventing languages. She feared that it would distract him from his studies, which might prevent him from winning a scholarship.

COUNTRY MOUSE, CITY SCHOLAR

In 1900, the Tolkiens were forced to say good-bye to Sarehole. Mabel and the boys hated to leave the beautiful countryside, but Ronald needed to start school. Because Ronald was too young to travel the 4 miles (6.4 km) alone to the city, the family decided to relocate to Birmingham. Leaving Sarehole was difficult for Ronald. He loved its trees and fields, its River Cole, and its spring meadows bursting with wildflowers.

Ronald also hated to leave the people of Sarehole and nearby Hall Green village. He found them both brave and kind. Later, he used these country people as models for the hobbits. In *The Hobbit* and *The Lord of the Rings*, Ronald described a peaceful country place that he named "The Shire." When he described Hobbiton, home of the hobbits, he was describing the green, rolling landscape of his childhood home.

Even though they were only separated by a few miles, two places could not have differed more than Sarehole and Birmingham. In 1900, nearly half a million people lived in the city of Birmingham. The city bustled with activity. Factories representing more than five hundred different industries spewed smoke into the sky. In the country, there had been an occasional horse cart on the street, but in Birmingham, many vehicles filled the streets. Ice wagons, coal wagons, and vegetable carts rumbled past. Sarehole remained quiet. Its air was pure. Its waters were clean.

Ronald, however, also benefited from the move. He enrolled in the best grammar school in Birmingham. What Ronald liked best about this school was that his father had attended it. To study there would connect him to his father's past.

Birmingham also offered many diversions. Ronald loved to explore its bookstores. On Paradise Street, the Tolkien brothers enjoyed clomping their boots on the original wooden pavement, which had been laid in

This button factory was one of thousands of industries in Birmingham at the beginning of the twentieth century. Buttons were manufactured from many materials, including bone, metal, glass, pearls, and animal horn.

1875. Violet sellers and herb merchants peddled their goods out of baskets. Street scavengers—usually poor, young boys without jobs—swept the streets searching for lost coins.

On Corporation Street, Ronald occasionally spotted a cyclist peddling past on a newfangled invention—a bicycle. Even more rarely, an early motorcar sputtered past. Downtown streets bustled with horse-drawn buses and carriages. Early steam trams, or streetcars, clattered past. Above their windows, huge signs advertised products such as custard powder.

A RELIGIOUS CONVERSION

Besides the move back to Birmingham, another major change for the family occurred in 1900. Mabel and her sister converted to Catholicism. This move shocked both families. Most of the Tolkiens and Suffields were Protestants. They disliked and distrusted Catholics. So strongly did they

Motorcars for the Masses

Birmingham became the center of Britain's fledgling automobile industry. In 1834, an early steam carriage built there carried forty passengers at a speed of 10 miles (16 km) an hour. The fact that hills did not slow it down amazed people. In the early 1900s, several firms began manufacturing petroleum-engine cars in Birmingham. One company switched from making sheep-shearing equipment to producing car engines. Although horse-drawn carriages still crowded Birmingham's streets, the tide was turning.

The lofty architecture of the Birmingham Oratory would have looked very familiar to Ronald. As a young student, he often served as an altar boy at one of its side altars.

feel, that after Mabel converted they cut off almost all financial support for the widow and her children. Even after her sister returned to her parents' faith, Mabel held firm. She refused to give up Catholicism.

The Tolkiens settled near the Birmingham Oratory, a church where many priests served. Ronald was baptized. Mabel became friends with a priest, Father Francis Xavier Morgan, whose family had come from Spain originally. Ronald loved to hear the priest speak the Spanish language. He decided to learn it.

Spanish was not the only new language Ronald studied in his first years of school. King Edward's School instructed its students in Latin and Greek. But it was another language that truly captured Ronald's imagination. One day near their small house by King's Heath Station, he discovered words that amazed him. They were painted on the sides of the railroad cars. These Welsh words struck Ronald as the most interesting and mysterious words he had ever seen. He could hardly wait to discover their meanings.

Welsh people call their language "the language of Heaven." All his life, Ronald considered Welsh to be the most beautiful language. He based his Sindarin language on it. In an essay called "English and Welsh," Ronald described what a change these Welsh words had made in his life. They had "pierced his linguistic heart."

In 1837, two architects, Augustus Pugin and Charles Barry, redesigned King Edward's School in the Gothic-revival style. This ornate style imitated the building style of the Middle Ages.

THREE

Animalic, Nevbosh, and Naffarin

Ronald entered King Edward VI High School for Boys in June of 1900. The school was located on New Street. King Edward's had recently opened a girl's school for the first time. However, young men and young women were educated separately. For that reason, all of Ronald's school chums were male.

The Guild of the Holy Cross, a Birmingham religious group, built the Free Grammar School in Birmingham in 1552. The school was named after King Henry VIII's son, King Edward VI. One unusual fact about the school's history was that the Duke of Northumberland, who was the lord mayor of Birmingham, was responsible for founding it during the

Reformation. The Act of Suppression of 1547 forced many schools to close because they were housed on the grounds of religious orders. During the Reformation, the English government set up the Church of England and closed many Catholic monasteries. So great was the duke's friendship with the king, that the king permitted The Guild of the Holy Cross to start a new school, even though he was closing many schools at the same time.

Later, King Edward's School began to charge fees. However, it always offered scholarships to talented children, regardless of whether they could afford to pay. When King Edward's first admitted Ronald, he had not yet secured a scholarship. Mabel quickly discovered that she could not afford the fees. In December of 1901, Ronald's mother withdrew him from the school. She sent him to St. Philip's, a nearby school. However, both mother and son soon realized that the Catholic school could not compare with King Edward's for excellence. Mabel urged Ronald to study even harder for a scholarship. In December of 1902, exactly one year after he had been forced to leave his father's school, Ronald won a Foundation Scholarship to King Edward's. The school renewed the scholarship in the years 1904, 1906, and 1908.

King Edward's School was situated in the heart of downtown Birmingham. In the 1880s and 1890s, Birmingham experienced a major building boom. Businesses of every description opened workshops downtown. When Ronald wandered down nearby alleys, he could find an iron bedstead maker, a brass founder, several jewel cutters, a paper box maker, and a gas lamp manufacturer. Big downtown stores advertised their latest attractions: modern elevators, mahogany counters, brass trim, and the latest in gas lighting. Arcades, or glass-roofed shops, offered toys and fancy goods from all over England.

In elementary school, Ronald studied all the required subjects: English, history, geography, arithmetic, mathematics, scripture, French, Latin, and drawing. So that all students would learn to appreciate the natural world, botany was also taught. The school also required all students to exercise in the gymnasium. Students could also elect to take courses in the arts, languages, and sciences.

FROM ANCIENT TONGUES TO INVENTED ONES

During his school years, Ronald continued to be fascinated by languages. Father Francis encouraged the boy's love of foreign words. The priest lent Ronald his own books so that the boy could practice Spanish. Ronald continued to learn Latin and Greek. What Ronald liked best about Greek was that it connected him to events that had occurred thousands of years ago.

Ronald also studied the history of his own language. At school, Ronald

This is a photograph of Tolkien's classroom in 1935. Tolkien sat on hard wooden benches like those pictured here. The relationship between students and teacher was much more formal than it is in schools today.

learned Middle English. This language was spoken in England from approximately 1150 to 1475. At home Ronald taught himself the language that people spoke in England even earlier. Anglo-Saxon, also known as Old English, was first spoken in the fifth century. Ronald learned that Anglo-Saxon had many "cousin" and "grandfather" languages. These languages included Old Norse, Old High German, Old Dutch, and Old Saxon, among others. Linguists, people who study languages, consider them all Germanic languages.

Most of these languages were no longer spoken. These so-called "dead languages" particularly fascinated Ronald. A school chum sold him a primer, or textbook, on the Gothic language. Goths had invaded and captured most of the Roman Empire in the third to the fifth centuries. Their language also belonged to the Germanic family of languages. "Gothic was the first to take me by storm, to move my heart," Ronald said in a speech called "English and Welsh." Later, as an adult, he wrote to the poet Auden that learning Gothic was the first time he studied "a language out of mere love." This love stayed with him for life. For years, Tolkien signed his names in his books in an elegant and old-fashioned Gothic script.

Ronald felt an intense pull toward the study of languages, but those from northern countries appealed to him the most. His daughter, Priscilla, wrote in an essay to honor the centenary (the hundred-year anniversary of her father's birth) that "at an early age his imagination had been stirred by northern civilizations."

Ronald's passionate interest in languages often caused him to ignore his lessons. In a 1968 interview in the *Daily Telegraph Magazine*, Ronald recalled how the study of new languages distracted him from his regular course work. "When I was supposed to be studying Latin and Greek, I studied Welsh and English. When I was supposed to be concentrating on English, I took up Finnish. . . ."

Some people thought that Ronald dwelled too much on dead tongues, but his friend, Christopher Wiseman, understood his passion for languages. Wiseman studied another ancient language. He was teaching himself to read hieroglyphics, which recorded the Middle Egyptian language.

In an interview in the London Sunday *Times* in November of 1966, an adult Tolkien described his feeling for his native tongue. "The language you are born into is a ready-made language, not a made-to-measure one. So you pull it about till you get it to fit you comfortably." But for Ronald, knowing one language was never enough. In the same *Times* interview, he recalled, "going on the train to Wales and seeing the name *Ebbw*. I couldn't get over it. Not long afterwards, I started inventing my own languages."

The Talk of the Nation

In North America, Sequoyah, a Cherokee Indian, created the first written Native American language. He was saddened because his people had no way to record special events the way other people did. Sequoyah decided to invent a system of writing. He substituted symbols for sounds. This is called a "syllabary" instead of an alphabet. Sequoyah described this new written language as "making the leaves talk."

FROM NONSENSE TO MEANING

Although Ronald did not claim to invent Animalic, it was the first invented language that he explored with friends. A simple language, Animalic words derived from the names for British birds, fish, and animals. In his essay on language invention, entitled "A Secret Vice," Ronald recalled his history with Animalic. "I was never fully instructed in it, nor a proper Animalic speaker. . ." In this speech, Ronald recalled a few words in Animalic: "*dog nightingale woodpecker forty . . .*"

Nevbosh was another story. Ronald did help to construct this language. The word "Nevbosh" meant "new nonsense." Ronald enjoyed communicating in a brand-new language with friends. But more than that, he loved hearing the new words spoken. He also loved making sense of them and stringing them together into sentences. In his speech "A Secret Vice," Ronald recalled his "horror at overhearing two entirely strange boys conversing in it." For Ronald, part of the attraction of inventing new languages was the secret communication they enabled.

His experiences with Animalic and Nevbosh made Ronald eager for a new challenge. What Ronald really desired, was to invent a new language from scratch. He knew that he could coin words based on existing languages easily. But could he create words without borrowing them from other tongues? When he was only eight or nine years old, Naffarin became the first language that Ronald worked on alone.

In an interview in *Seventeen Magazine* in January of 1967, Ronald recalled exactly how he invented a new language. "Well the way I did it was to start with *p-t-k*. Then of course you get *b-d-g*, and then the nasals— *mm—nn—nng* . . . and on and on and eventually there's your language."

There are countless ways to develop a new language. As a young child, Ronald filled page after page with possibilities.

His language invention took many, many hours. Ronald's mother, who always wanted him to concentrate on his schoolwork, noticed that he was spending time during which he should have been doing homework on his word play. Repeatedly, she warned him that he needed to keep his scholarship. So to please his mother, Ronald destroyed all his first attempts at language invention. Later, he regretted that he could never page through them again.

At school, Ronald studied how several languages—German, French, Celtic, and Latin—had influenced modern English. Influence was too mild a word. The languages of invaders and locals, of government and religion, had clashed violently. From this molten, pressurized stew, a new language, English, had formed. English arrived in Britain on the tongues of warriors. The Angles, Jutes, and Saxons, three Germanic tribes, forced the native Britons to move westward. So powerful was the spread of this new language that only about twenty words from Celtic (the language of the native Britons) survived into Old English. Since then English has borrowed words from many languages, including Latin, French, Japanese, and Sanskrit.

One fancy new word Ronald learned from his schoolmasters was "philology." Philology means the study of languages. It comes from two Greek words: *philein*, to love, and *logos*, word. Philologists study ancient texts. They do so to discover their meanings and to try to understand what life was like during earlier times. Even in grade school, Ronald had decided that philology would be central to his life.

Several of Ronald's instructors at King Edward's recognized the boy's great talent for languages. George Brewerton, in particular, encouraged the boy. He gave Ronald a book on learning Anglo-Saxon. Brewerton's enthusiasm for tracing words back to the past matched Ronald's own.

When Brewerton saw how much Ronald loved the author Chaucer, he recommended other early English works of literature. Ronald loved myths and tales that featured dragons. Many of these legends were written in Old Norse, not in English. To learn more about northern myths, Ronald began the study of Old Norse. By the time he graduated from King Edward's School Ronald had studied nine languages: Latin, French, Greek, Spanish, Celtic, Welsh, Old Norse, Anglo-Saxon, and English. Some of these he knew fluently. Others he studied merely for pleasure.

A MYSTERIOUS DISEASE

When he was twelve years old, Ronald's mother began to suffer from frightening symptoms. She had headaches. Often, she felt extremely thirsty. She grew thinner and thinner and became very weak. Some days, she was so ill that she could not get out of bed. Eventually, a physician diagnosed

A Taste of Honey

A British physician first connected diabetes mellitus to a problem with blood sugar. Dr. Thomas Willis discovered this relationship in a bizarre way. In 1670, he tasted his patient's urine in a chamber pot. He reported that it tasted as sweet as honey. That is how the disease received the second part of its name. In Latin, *mellitus* means "honey."

that she had diabetes mellitus. The word *diabetes* comes from the Greek language. It means "siphon." To "siphon" means "to flow out." The ancient Greeks named the disease this because people who suffered from it drank huge quantities of water and had to relieve themselves often.

When Mabel grew ill with diabetes, her doctors advised bed rest. Father Francis arranged for her to rest in a place in the country. He chose Rednal, a small village outside of Birmingham. Mabel and the boys spent a wonderful summer there. During that summer Mabel improved. The boys enjoyed playing outside in the forests and fields again.

However in the fall, Mabel grew sick again. Even though her physicians understood that she had a problem regulating the sugar in her blood, they had no medicine that could help her. Five years earlier, two German scientists, Von Miring and Minnows, had proved that the pancreas produced insulin. But it was not until 1921 that someone invented a method for manufacturing insulin. That was too late for Ronald's mother. One day that autumn, Mabel collapsed suddenly. She fell into a coma and died on November 14, 1904. Ronald and his brother became orphans.

FOUR

Tea Clubs and Poetry

In her will, Mabel appointed Father Francis to be the boys' guardian. She knew that her family would not raise her sons as Catholics. The priest proved to be a fortunate choice. He was intelligent and kind. What's more, Ronald and Hilary liked him very much. Because he was a priest, the boys could not live with him, but each summer, he took them on long vacations to the coast.

Father Francis found an aunt of the brothers who ran a boarding house. The aunt did not object to Catholicism the way most of the other relatives did. After his mother's death, Ronald felt even more committed to Catholicism. He felt that his mother had died young because of their poverty, which he blamed on his relatives' negative response to his mother's faith.

This aunt, Beatrice Suffield, agreed to care for the boys. For nearly four years, Ronald and Hilary lived with her. During this time, the brothers kept very close ties to the oratory. They served as altar boys for morning mass. Afterwards, they shared breakfast with the learned priests.

Aunt Beatrice seemed distant to the boys. Hilary adapted to life with her, but Ronald felt sad living in such a cold atmosphere. One day, Ronald discovered that his aunt had burned all his mother's letters. On a summer vacation with the priest, Ronald complained. Father Francis found the boys a new home. Mrs. Faulkner offered lodging on Duchess Road for area orphans. The boys moved in. To Ronald's great delight, a girl with short brown hair and grey eyes lived directly below them on the first floor. She was three years older than Ronald and almost grown-up.

Learning Circa 1900

By the time he turned thirteen, Ronald had to make a major decision: whether to study in the modern or the classical department at his school. The modern tract included courses in the sciences, whereas the classical tract concentrated on ancient languages. Ronald did not think twice. He chose the classical tract.

Edith Bratt had been orphaned as well. When Edith was fourteen years old, her mother had died. Relatives sent her to the Dresden House School. The Watts sisters, who owned the school, taught her classical piano. She practiced for hours every day and decided to make a career playing the piano.

Edith came to Faulkner's house because they both shared a great love of music. Faulkner often hosted musical evenings. She needed someone to play piano for her guests. Edith's guardian heard that this landlady, who was fond of music, needed a boarder. However, although Faulkner encouraged Edith to play for all her parties, she did not like when Edith played the piano for herself. So in the end, it was not the best living situation for a young woman who loved to play music.

Edith called Faulkner the "Old Lady." After noticing how the brothers seemed hungry most of the time, Edith devised a plan. She coaxed a kitchen servant to steal extra portions for the boys. The servant sent these upstairs to Edith's room on a dumbwaiter, which is a small elevator used to transport food or dishes between floors. Edith and the boys rigged up a rope outside their windows. Whenever a new basket of food arrived, Edith tugged the rope to signal that a snack was on its way.

Eventually, Faulkner found out. By that time Edith and Ronald had become close friends. They took cycling trips together and met in shops for tea. They exchanged presents on each other's birthdays. In time, someone who knew Father Francis spotted Edith and Ronald together and reported to the priest that the young couple were spending time with each other away from the boarding house.

Ronald's guardian advised him that he was too young to have a serious girlfriend. The fact that Edith was Protestant did not help matters. Just as his mother had warned him years before to concentrate on his studies, Father Francis used the same argument now. Soon, Ronald would need to take the scholarship examination for Oxford University. Competition would be keen. To separate the couple, Father Francis moved the brothers to other lodgings. He asked Ronald to break off his relationship with Edith.

Ronald loved Edith. She meant more to him than anyone except his brother, but he also admired Father Francis. He felt extremely grateful for all that the priest had done for him and Hilary. He knew also that Father Francis was right. Edith would distract him from his studies. In fact, he failed in his first attempt at the scholarship examination. Still, he cared deeply for Edith. He told the priest that he would not see her, yet eventually he did. When Ronald was caught again, Father Francis made Ronald promise that he would not see or write to Edith until he came of legal age.

This is Mr. A. E. Measure's House Group. Tolkien is seated in the front row, second from left, next to the teacher. In British schools a house group is a community of students who compete in sporting events and other activities against other house groups in the school.

In a letter to his son, Michael, written in 1941, Ronald recalled the desperate situation he found himself that winter of 1910. Ronald explained that he had to decide between deceiving Father Francis and ending his relationship with Edith. For Ronald it was an extremely difficult decision. But at eighteen, he knew he was too young to marry. He did not think that it would be fair to ask Edith to promise anything when they would spend the next three years apart. Edith moved in with friends far away in Cheltenham, while Ronald prepared to take his scholarship examination again.

TEA DRINKERS

At King Edward's School, Ronald became active in clubs and teams. He played rugby. He wrote for the school newspaper and joined the debating society. One topic Ronald discussed in debate was the suffragettes. These activists were pressing the government to give women the right to vote. During another debate, according to biographer Humphrey Carpenter, Ronald achieved some fame around the school. He played the part of a Greek ambassador to the Roman senate. He argued forcibly in Greek. Then switching roles in the middle of the debate, he played a barbarian. Everyone was amazed to hear him continue the debate in fluent Gothic.

At King Edward's, Ronald formed a club. He named it the Tea Club because the members secretly shared tea in the school library. Of course, drinking in the library was not allowed. However, several of the boys, as the oldest students in the school, were in charge of the library and let it happen. Ronald invited a few friends to join the club.

Although any and all topics were game for discussion, the young men usually shared their opinions of literary works. Within this circle of friends, Ronald began a lifelong tradition of forming clubs with other men to discuss literature.

The Tea Club included only a few students. The main ones were Ronald, Christopher Wiseman, and Rob Gilson, who was the headmaster's son. During examination week, the boys had to leave school between exams to buy lunch. They met downtown at Barrow's Store. After a while, a fourth regular member, G. B. Smith, joined the group. Wiseman recalled in a 1987 oral history interview how they used to meet at a long table in a narrow area of the tea shop. Because of its shape, they nicknamed their meeting space "the railway carriage."

Once they started holding meetings downtown, they added "Barrovian Society" to their name after the store in which they met. The club became known as the Tea Club, Barrovian Society, or T. C. B. S. At meetings, Ronald read aloud from *Beowulf* and shared Norse sagas with his friends. Other members shared modern poetry. Besides literature, they also discussed science and art.

Heroic Tales

In the Icelandic language, the word *saga* means "what is said or told." Icelandic sagas were recorded between 1190 and 1320. They were handed down from generation to generation as spoken tales. Sagas report many tragedies, as well as deeds of heroism, battles, and great adventures.

ON POEMS AND JEWELS

Ronald began to write poetry seriously during his last year at King Edward's School. He loved to read poems at the Tea Club meetings. Ronald would sometimes ask other members for feedback on his writing. Later, at Oxford, he shared a new poem with Christopher Wiseman. According to biographer Humphrey Carpenter, Wiseman suggested that Ronald not try to jam everything he knew into one poem. He told Ronald that his poem had so much in it that it reminded him of a lady who felt compelled to wear every single piece of jewelry she owned.

During those years, Ronald first discovered the topics that would interest him for the rest of his life. For instance, he found himself drawn to old Anglo-Saxon poems. In one poem, which dates back to the early history of the English language, he found a reference to Earendil, a ray or bright light. Ronald later used this image in his book *The Silmarillion*. In that book, the ship *Earendil* becomes the brightest star in heaven.

Goblins, gnomes, leprechauns, and elves inhabited Ronald's poems. He did not write poetry set in the modern world, but in a legendary world of long ago, where fantastic creatures roamed. The settings were often forest glades. Poetry became a lifelong passion. His last book, *The Simarillion,* includes both poetry and prose. In poetry, Ronald first captured his imagined world of long ago with all its fantastic, wonderful creatures.

Edith, to whom Father Francis had permitted Ronald to write to again, encouraged Ronald's poetry. She requested that Ronald make up poems about trees, flowers, and little elves. To please Edith, he wrote the following poems: "The Man in the Moon Came Down Too Soon," "Goblin Feet," and "The Shores of Faery."

MOUNTAIN SPIRITS

The year Ronald graduated from King Edward's School, his guardian awarded him a special present—a walking tour of Switzerland. Hilary and a group of family friends accompanied him. Around the turn of the twentieth century, a summer hiking trip in the Swiss mountains was often a right of passage for English youth. Winston Churchill, who later became prime minister of Great Britain, took a similar walking tour in 1893.

Except for the great sea voyages of his early childhood, Ronald seldom went on journeys. Yet each trip he undertook affected him greatly. For her father's centenary tribute, his daughter Priscilla wrote, "Although my father traveled relatively little, he had the capacity to be deeply stirred and excited by new experiences."

Years after he returned home from Switzerland, Ronald wrote about the magnificent vistas he saw in the Alps. He remembered the dramatic

Dangerous Elevations

Tolkien's near-death experience while climbing in the Alps left him with a lifelong respect for the hazards of mountain travel. In *The Hobbit*, he described stone giants heaving boulders at each other. In *The Lord of the Rings* trilogy, the hobbits and their friends find the Misty Mountains almost impossible to cross. Mortal dangers abounded on both their craggy peaks and in the deep caves below. So dangerous were these mountains that it was said that they had been created by Morgoth, the Dark Foe.

glaciers and crevasses that had fascinated him that summer. He used these still vivid memories to describe the Misty Mountains in *The Lord of the Rings.*

In a 1967 letter to his son Michael, Ronald recalled one of the great adventures of his Swiss trip. Ronald and his party were hiking up the Aletsch Glacier when an event occurred that almost caused his death. Ronald described being boxed in on a trail that was bordered on the left by a deep ravine and on the right by a steep slope that rose up the mountain. On the narrow path above them stood piles of rocks and boulders. The day was warm and the sun melted the snow. Without warning, many of the rocks broke free. They began to zoom toward them at frightening speeds. One boulder just missed striking the hiker in front of Ronald. She jumped out of the way. The rock missed Ronald by mere inches.

Front Quad at Exeter College shows the uniqueness of each college at Oxford. Each college owns its buildings and has its own faculty and students.

FIVE

From Quenya to Secret Code

Ronald applied for a scholarship to Oxford, one of the best universities in the world. On his first attempt, he did not secure one. When he took the examination again, he won an Exhibition Scholarship. This award disappointed Ronald's teachers. They knew he could have received a much better scholarship if he had worked harder. Ronald agreed that he was "one of the idlest boys" that Headmaster Gilson ever taught. At least the Exhibition Scholarship would cover most of his college costs.

The city of Oxford lies at the meeting place of two rivers, the Thames and the Cherwell. Full of towers, spires, and medieval courtyards, the city is quite beautiful.

The poet John Keats, one of the university's most famous graduates, praised the school's magnificent setting.

The university is divided into thirty-five separate colleges. Exeter, Ronald's college, opened in 1314. Walter de Stapeldon, the Bishop of Exeter and Treasurer of England, founded the college. He wanted to educate ministers for his parishes.

Exeter assigned Ronald rooms in Swiss Cottage. In an odd stroke of fate, Ronald's son, John, lived in this same building a generation later.

When Ronald went to Oxford in 1911, the university enforced many rules. Gates were locked each night. After hours, no student could leave campus. Cold baths were required. All students had to attend chapel services except for Catholics, Jews, and Nonconformists—Protestants who did not belong to the Anglican Church. Because Ronald was Catholic, he could worship at his own church instead.

During Eights Week, boaters race on the River Isis through Oxford. The most exciting part of the race is watching boats bump into each other. After a successful bump, the crew moves up to a higher place in the line-up for the next day's race.

Freshmen received the nickname Freshers. Freshers and upperclassmen often played mischievous practical jokes. Many of these jokes were directed against other students, but town residents received their share. Students dressed in black gowns whenever they attended lectures and even had to wear them when they left campus. Because of this, students received the nickname Gowners, while the local residents were called Towners.

Oxford students had a great tradition of coining names for every possible kind of student. If you studied hard, you became known as a scholar. Toshers came from poorer families than commoners, who despite their name, actually came from higher-class families. Writer Joan McCluskey described some of the other kinds of students: "Academically, a student could be a fop [a student who didn't know anything but pretended he knew a great deal], or a swot [someone who really cared for academics a great deal]. A heartie was an athletic type, friendly and outgoing. . . . Tolkien was a scholar, a swot, and a heartie."

Intense competition developed between colleges. Students often hurled insults over neighboring walls. Sometimes, they teased each other with songs they made up on the spot. Ronald joined in the fun. During his first semester, he stole a city bus. He piloted his friends on a joyride through Oxford's streets. Amazingly, Ronald received no punishment for this serious prank.

IN LANGUAGE DEEP

Suprisingly, between his busy social life and watching punters (or boaters) on the river, Ronald found time to study. He decided to focus on the Latin and Greek Languages. Oxonians, or Oxford students, called this course of study "Greats." Traditionally, students chose "Greats" to prepare for careers in law, politics, or the civil service. Later, Ronald switched courses. He wanted to spend more time learning Old English and other northern European languages. He wanted to study original texts in those languages. He joined the new Department of English Language and Literature and chose Comparative Philology for his major course of study.

One professor greatly encouraged Ronald's study of languages. Professor Wright also influenced Ronald's choice of careers. This philologist shared Tolkien's fascination with languages from the past, including Gothic. In fact, he had written the Gothic primer that Ronald had treasured so much as a boy.

Because of extreme poverty in his family, the odds of Joseph Wright becoming a professor were almost zero. Even a poor orphan, such as Ronald, had a better chance. So poor had Wright been that as a young child, he'd lived in a workhouse with the poorest of the poor. At age six, young Wright began work as a donkey-boy for a blacksmith. Wright

No Women Allowed

Until modern times, British universities did not allow women to enroll as students. The universities had developed from monasteries. For centuries, they enforced a males-only policy. In 1832, the University of London allowed female students to enroll, but it was not until World War I that Oxford welcomed female students in large numbers. Oxford graduated its first female students in 1920.

hauled tools between Woodend Quarry and the nearest blacksmith. Each of the quarrymen paid Wright one penny.

Later, the seven-year-old Wright worked many hours each day in Sir Titus Salt's Mill in Saltaire. Wright never attended a full day of school in his life. When he could, he visited his school class. This barely helped. After several years, Joseph left grammar school, but he could neither read nor write.

When the Franco-Prussian War struck, Wright, now a teenager, over-heard other mill workers reading battle accounts aloud. These readings inspired him to begin night classes. He learned basic reading and then began to study French. Later, he studied German. Within a few years, he began his own night school to teach other poor workers how to read. Eventually, Wright learned how to speak thirteen languages.

Wright recognized Ronald's great talent for words. He urged him to continue studying Britain's old languages: Anglo-Saxon and Middle English. He also encouraged Ronald to keep working on his invented tongues.

Wright also advised Ronald to continue reading myths and epic poems in their original languages. Myths retell the stories of gods, heroes, and supermen. Ronald studied the works of Chaucer and the poem *Beowulf*. Scholars consider this poem to be an epic. An epic is a very long poem that details the deeds of heroes in the past. *Beowulf*, which dates from the eighth century, is the oldest English epic poem. Some experts compare *Beowulf* to the *Iliad* or *Odyssey* of Greek literature.

Ronald read *Beowulf* in the original Anglo-Saxon language. He especially enjoyed the description of Grendel, the giant monster that ate fifteen Danish warriors in the Danish king's great hall. Grendel also snatched fifteen more warriors to drag back to his marshy lair. This epic reminded Ronald of the dragon stories his mother had read to him so long ago.

Ronald loved discovering familiar words in the Anglo-Saxon poem. He recognized *lif, man, hus* immediately as "life," "man," and "house." He also found words that had changed slightly more over the centuries, such as *moder, hond, swearde,* and *worulde.* These words are spelled now "mother," "hand," "sword," and "world."

Ronald felt himself drawn more and more to northern myths and legends. While still at King Edward's, he read a translation from Finnish of the *Kalevala.* The *Kalevala* is a mythological account of Finland's early history. Ronald wished that England had a similar myth of its own, something that would celebrate England's heroic past.

While studying for an honors examination in 1912, Ronald found a Finnish grammar book in the library stacks. Instead of continuing to study for his important examination, Ronald began to translate this Finnish epic on his own. His old habit of surrendering himself totally to a new language at

English Poet Extraordinaire

Chaucer lived during exciting times. He survived the Black Plague, which struck England in 1348, when he was about eight years old. French soldiers captured him during the Hundred Years War. The king of England ransomed him. He went to Italy just before two rival popes fought over control of the Catholic Church. After his wife, Philippa, died in 1367, Chaucer wrote *The Canterbury Tales.*

the expense of whatever else he was supposed to be doing at the moment had resurfaced again. His love for Finnish inspired him to begin inventing a new language. Eventually, he called this language Quenya or High Elvish. Ronald said later that Latin, Finnish, and Greek all influenced his Quenyan language. Most of its grammar came from Finnish. When he showed this new language to Wright, the professor urged him to keep working on it.

A BROKEN ENGAGEMENT

At midnight on the day he turned twenty-one, Ronald wrote to Edith Bratt. He asked when they could meet again. Her response shocked him. She replied that she had gotten engaged to another man. She planned to marry a farmer named George Field. He was the brother of a schoolmate.

As an orphan herself, Edith had to think of her future. She had no family to rely on for financial help. In those days, most professions were closed to women. The Jessops, the friends with whom she lived in Cheltenham, were pressuring her to get married. On January 21, Edith would turn twenty-four. Her friends warned her to find a husband before it was too late.

Although Ronald had written to her throughout the previous three years, he had kept his promise to Father Francis. He had not discussed matters of love. Besides, he and Edith came from very different religious backgrounds. Mr. Jessop, like many British of his class at that time, felt an intense dislike for Catholics.

Ronald had written to Edith on January 3. On January 8, he boarded a train to go visit her in Cheltenham. By the end of the afternoon, he convinced Edith to marry him instead. Still, Ronald and Edith decided not to tell their family or friends. They knew that most would disapprove. In fact, when her engagement to Ronald became known, Edith had to leave the Jessop home. But their happiness at having found each other again would help them overcome all obstacles that faced them.

SIX

In the Shadow of War

The Great War, or World War I as it is now called, began during the summer vacation of 1914. Overnight, life changed dramatically at Oxford. Posters appeared everywhere with a picture of a soldier pointing at the viewer. "*JOIN YOUR COUNTRY'S ARMY!*" the text read. By the end of September, more than two thousand Oxford students had enlisted. Many fellows, or professors, signed up as well. T. E. Lawrence, an Oxford don, or teacher, journeyed east with the army. Later, he achieved fame as Lawrence of Arabia. When college servants enlisted, the university agreed to pay the difference in their wages.

Tolkien decided to complete his course work. Now that graduation was within sight, he hated to depart without receiving a degree. But things had changed. Instead of spending long hours reading Icelandic sagas at tea shops with friends, Ronald now practiced military drills with the Officers'

Training Corps. Within months, the listings next to many students' names changed from "A" (absent) to "D" (deceased).

In 1915, Tolkien was one of only two students at Exeter College to graduate with a first class degree in English Language and Literature. His special subject was Old Icelandic. This degree, along with a specialty in Greek philology, which he had earned in 1911, would help Tolkien secure a teaching position after the war.

A QUIET WEDDING

Tolkien enlisted in the Thirteenth Reserve Battalion of the Lancashire Fusiliers in July of 1915. In doing this, Tolkien took an unusual step. Normally, men joined their hometown's battalion. Tolkien's good friend and former T. C. B. S.

This is one of many posters that encouraged young British men to enlist to serve in World War I. There was no draft, so the government had to actively recruit volunteers.

AN APPEAL TO YOU

member, G. B. Smith, had enlisted at the same time, so Tolkien chose the Lancashire Fusiliers, Smith's hometown battalion. As usual, with Tolkien, friendship came first. However, this plan backfired. The army assigned Tolkien and Smith to separate units.

Because many men never returned from the front—almost one million British soldiers died during the war—Tolkien and Edith decided to marry before Ronald left for France. Reluctantly, Edith's guardian, Stephen Gamely, gave his consent. He feared that Tolkien would never earn a decent living. Edith's friend "Uncle" Jessop agreed. According to Priscilla and John Tolkien in a *Tolkien Family Album,* Uncle Jessop, said "I have nothing to say against Tolkien, he is a cultured [gentleman], but his prospects are poor in the extreme, and when he will be in a position to marry I can not imagine."

Tolkien visited his guardian, Father Francis. The young man requested control of his small inheritance. He wanted to invite the priest to the wedding, but he remembered how strongly Father Francis had opposed his relationship with Edith. So he kept quiet about his plans. Two weeks before

Trench Warfare

A French engineer named Sébastian de Vauban developed a system of trench warfare in the seventeenth century. World War I was fought primarily in these "ribbons of death" in Europe. Opposing armies dug trenches less than one rifle shot apart. Soldiers nicknamed the dangerous space between "No Man's Land." When the war began, the British army owned 2,500 shovels. By war's end, the army possessed more than 10 million.

the wedding, he sent the priest an invitation. Father Francis replied joyfully that he would love to say the wedding vows, but Tolkien and Edith had already made other arrangements.

Edith and Tolkien married on March 22, 1916, at a Catholic church in Warwick. They chose a Wednesday for the ceremony because they had reunited on that day of the week back in 1913. Less than three months after the wedding, Tolkien received his orders to join the fighting. On June 6, 1916, Tolkien boarded a ship at Calais that was bound for France.

WAR TO END ALL WARS

Tolkien seldom discussed the war. Although he often remarked that it had no influence on his writing, his friend and fellow writer, C. S. Lewis, strongly disagreed. Lewis believed that Tolkien based much of *The Lord of the Rings* on his war experiences. What Tolkien captured about the war, Lewis said, was that eerie, threatening silence before battles. Tolkien also

The Night the War Paused

A very unusual event happened one night in 1914. Soldiers on both sides of the lines, German, French, English, and Belgian, sang carols to each other on Christmas Eve. The next day they buried their dead together and then shared holiday meals. They even played soccer. When first ordered to fight again, they aimed their rifles overhead. For a few short days, peace reigned.

recorded in his books the comfort given by other soldiers, and the surprising joy found in small things.

For the rest of his life, Ronald felt a strong distaste for war. He remembered the French front as "miles and miles of seething, tortured earth." He fought at the Somme, one of the bloodiest battles in history. The British suffered about 58,000 casualties—more than 19,000 dead and the rest wounded—on the battle's first day. It was the bloodiest single day of World War I.

Two aspects of the war affected Tolkien for the rest of his life. The first was that it made him keenly aware of the world's beauty. The second saddened him very much. In the war, he lost all of his childhood friends except for one. Only Christopher Wiseman, another T.C.B.S. member, survived.

IN A HOLE IN THE GROUND, SOLDIERS

During World War I, the British army censored many letters that the soldiers mailed home. They did this to prevent vital military information from being discovered by the enemy. Censors scissored open letters. They either inked out passages or cut them out of the letters entirely. What they searched for were passages that mentioned where soldiers were stationed, how many fought in a unit, or other information of that type. They confiscated, or seized, letters that they felt told too much of this vital information.

Because of this censorship, Ronald and Edith developed their own private code for keeping track of where Tolkien was stationed. Each time Ronald moved, he planted a secret series of dots in the letter. Translating these dots, Edith marked her husband's new battle station on a map of

France. This helped the newlyweds feel close, despite the miles that separated them.

Tolkien worked with other codes as well during those war months. Because of his great ability with languages, he received training as a signaler. He learned Morse Code and the ancient system of using signal flags. Greek warriors first used flags to transmit messages. Tolkien trained pigeons to send messages because in the trenches, bombs tore many of the telephone lines out of the ground.

If the war had not been waged outside, trench life might have been bearable. Soldiers dug trenches as deep as 20 feet (6 m) below the ground. Others built steps into them. Some lucky soldiers slept in wire cots underground. Braziers, or small heaters, kept them warm.

When the rains came, the situation grew horrible. Newspapers reported that the soldiers turned into "statues of clay." Sometimes the mud grew so thick that infantrymen disappeared into it and were never found

To Mexico With Love

One of history's most famous cases of code breaking occurred during World War I. In 1917, Germany sent Mexico a secret message, asking its government to enter the war on the German side. To repay Mexico for fighting against the United States, Germany promised that they would help Mexico reclaim New Mexico and Arizona after the war. Unfortunately for Germany, British codebreakers cracked this code. They informed the U.S. government. Soon after this German cable was understood, the United States entered the war against Germany.

again. The year before Tolkien arrived in France, fifteen British soldiers drowned in a trench. Engineers built the trenches in zigzags, so that shock waves from the exploding artillery shells would not travel across them and kill more men.

For the rest of his life, Tolkien recalled the destruction caused by World War I. In *Surprised by Joy*, his friend C. S. Lewis recalled his similar experiences with trench warfare. "The horribly smashed men still moving like half-crushed beetles, the sitting or standing corpses, the landscape of sheer earth without a blade of grass, the boots worn day and night till they seemed to grow to your feet. . . ."

In the trenches, soldiers had to learn quickly how to tell the difference between artillery shot and machine gun fire. They needed to identify the whish of German "sausage" mortar shells as they whizzed overhead. Sometimes, by recognizing a sound, a soldier could save his or a comrade's life.

These British soldiers of the East Lancashire Regiment used a periscope to check on the enemy's progress. A periscope is an optical instrument with lenses, mirrors, and a long tube that allows you to see above the ground.

In the end, fighting in the trenches probably saved Tolkien's life. While living in those tunnels, he caught trench fever. This disease caused life-threatening fevers that did not go away for months.

Tolkien was sent to a hospital in Birmingham. Edith came to nurse him. Shortly before Christmas, he received a letter from Christopher Wiseman informing him of G. B. Smith's death. According to biographer, Humphrey Carpenter, earlier that fall, Smith had written Tolkien, "May God bless you, my dear John Ronald, and may you say the things I have tried to say long after I am not there to say them, if such be my lot."

SEVEN

From Hospital Elves
to Forest Muses

The deaths of G. B. Smith and Rob Gilson from the Tea Club, Barrovian Society convinced Tolkien that he must devote his life to something important. The members of the T. C. B. S. held their last meeting during the Christmas holidays of 1914. The four men decided then that they had joined together for something even more vital than friendship.

During World War I, the deaths of his talented comrades convinced Tolkien that he must create something in their honor. After his friend Gilson died in 1916, Tolkien wrote G. B. Smith that the young men of the T. C. B. S. had shared a special spirit that must continue. Tolkien felt that whoever survived the war must do something important. Whatever work they might do would owe its inspiration to the friendship of the four young men. Ironically, G. B. Smith died soon afterward.

While his body was healing from the fever that he had contracted in France, Tolkien's mind worked actively. He knew that whatever work he chose must include his invented languages. His study of the *Kalevala*, the Finnish epic, convinced him that his languages must consist of more than words and rules of grammar. He realized that he wanted to do something much larger than constructing new vocabularies. He wanted to create a web of legends.

Of Lice and Men

For most of World War I, doctors did not understand why so many soldiers were contracting a strange, intense fever. They termed the condition PUO or pyrexia, unknown origin. Pyrexia means fever. Not until 1918, the last year of the war, did doctors determine that lice in the trenches transmitted this horrible disease from soldier to soldier.

Later, Tolkien described this vision in a letter to Milton Waldman. He told his friend that he had decided "to make a body of more or less connected legend . . . which I could dedicate simply to: to England; to my country. . . ."

Tolkien spent most of 1917 in and out of hospitals. His trench fever improved, but then flared up again. He carried his notebooks with him even while in the hospital. Tolkien began to jot down stories now which included elves, fairies, and dwarfs.

During those weeks of rest and healing, Tolkien decided that not only would his writings include his invented languages, but they would also be tied to mythology. Just as the unnamed author or authors of the *Kalevala* described the legends of the Finnish people, his writings would invent legends for his own people, the people of the West Midlands in England.

By writing down these tales, Tolkien could bring together all his talents and interests. He could combine his love for the fairy tales and myths of his youth, his language play, his years of language study, his practice of poetry, and his Oxford education in philology. From these varied ingredients, Tolkien would create legends.

On November 17, 1917, Edith gave birth to a son. They named him John Reuel. Reuel had been Tolkien's father's middle name. Tolkien's brother Hilary shared this name as well. Now Ronald and Edith passed it on to a new generation. In Hebrew, Reuel means "friend of God." So highly did the Tolkiens value this name that all four of their children received it as a middle name. They even bestowed it on Priscilla, their only daughter.

In between hospital visits, Tolkien and Edith traveled. At one point, they spent time near a forest on the Holderness Peninsula in northeast England. One day Edith danced in a field of hemlock flowers. Seeing his wife twirl amid the flowers inspired Ronald to write a poem.

He wrote about Tinuviel dancing among the hemlock flowers. In later years, Tolkien would change Tinuviel's name to Lúthien. As "The Song of Beren and Lúthien," this poem appeared in *The Lord of the Rings.* In this early poem, Tolkien celebrated his love for his wife. Edith encouraged Tolkien's writing. In between practicing the piano, she copied out her husband's stories and poems. She was his main audience at that point.

MIDDLE-EARTH

Tolkien had no interest in writing about the modern world. He hated machines. He hated war. His beautiful Sarehole countryside was being ripped apart by machines. Factories replaced meadows. Roads and houses replaced trees and fields. Black and sooty Birmingham had begun to overrun Sarehole, the land most precious to Tolkien on earth.

Ronald wanted to write about the past; a past where trees and flowers still graced the landscape and fairies might have flittered past. Tolkien wanted to construct a world similar to the magical, green island that he had journeyed to as a child from a distant land across the sea. He wanted to celebrate the brave men who had fought during the war. He wanted to pay homage to the simple, honest country people he had met as a child in Sarehole. Most of all, after all the senseless death he had witnessed, he wanted to celebrate life.

The woods and marshes of Sarehole would remain Tolkien's lifelong idea of beauty, long after they were torn down, long after the city of Birmingham swallowed up this peaceful country village.

As Tolkien thought about where to set his new tales, he remembered the Middle English word *middangeand* that he had learned at Oxford, which meant "middle-earth." Tolkien recognized that Middle-earth was the world he had been searching for, the only world that would engage his imagination. Tolkien planned to fill Middle-earth with heroic men and mythical creatures.

In 1917, Tolkien wrote the first story of his mythology. "The Fall of Gondolin" tells how evil Morgoth attacks the High Elves to steal their jewels. Ronald spent many hours working on an Elvish word list. The Elvish language was the same Quenyan tongue Tolkien had invented in college. Tolkien would work on this language for the rest of his life. According to his son, Christopher, Quenya was the language closest to his heart. He wrote some sections of *The Lord of the Rings* and *The Silmarillion* in Quenya. Tolkien once said that he wished he could write more of his stories in this language.

BLESSED BY FEVER

Complications from trench fever kept Ronald away from the battlefront for the rest of the war. Trench fever differs from most fevers, because it can recur again and again. Some patients suffer a recurrence of the fever eight or nine times. It also lasts longer than other fevers—up to nearly a week at a time. Even more dangerous, the fever can reach a life-threatening 105 degrees Fehrenheit (40.8 degrees Celsius). Other complications include severe weakness, dizziness, rashes, and intense pain in the back and the legs.

The other members of Tolkien's battalion who remained at the front were either killed or captured during the war. Tolkien, however, could not shake his illness. His fever might break, but then it would return.

At one point he did get better. He was told to go back to the trenches. Shortly before he was scheduled to report for duty, his fever returned. Illness brought luck to Tolkien. Trench fever brought him back to England, where Edith nursed him. His long hospital stays provided him with more free time than he would have for the rest of his life. He used this time to write and make up languages.

By October 1918, it appeared that the war would end very soon. Tolkien traveled to Oxford to look for work. Because of the war, Oxford had few students left. Only about 360 students remained compared to the more than 3,000 students that had attended the colleges in 1914. University officials could not offer Tolkien a job because they didn't know what the post-war years would bring. They would have to wait and see.

One contact at Oxford proved more rewarding. Tolkien's former Icelandic tutor, William Craigie, offered him a position working on the *New English Dictionary*. For a young Oxford graduate to work on the world's most famous dictionary was a great honor. When the war ended on November 11, 1918, Tolkien returned to Oxford. After all the horror and suffering he'd seen, Tolkien was happy to return to the safe harbor of language.

After working on the Oxford dictionary, Sir William Craigie visited the United States, where he edited a four-volume American dictionary.

EIGHT

Walrus to Leeds

When the *New English Dictionary* was completed in 1928, the first copies were presented to King George V of England and President Calvin Coolidge of the United States. So highly did the British value this work that Craigie, the man who had hired Tolkien, was granted a knightship. He became Sir William Craigie.

Languages constantly change. New words are added and old words disappear. Because of this, new editions of dictionaries are always necessary. But revising a dictionary is a monumental task. Each entry requires an enormous amount of detailed labor. Tolkien's work for the *New English Dictionary* consisted of three main tasks. He had to research the meaning, pronunciation, and history of each word.

Today, the *New English Dictionary* is known as the *Oxford English Dictionary*, or the OED. Scholars recognize it as the best dictionary of the

English language. When Tolkien was hired in 1918, the staff had been struggling for years to complete the task. They had made much progress. By the time Tolkien joined the staff, they had reached the "Ws."

The work had begun in 1879. The original editor, James A. H. Murray, had promised to finish the entire dictionary in ten years. After five years, he had only reached the word "Ant." To arrive at "W" was a major achievement. "Zymotic" and "zymurgy" were in sight.

Tolkien loved the work. Instead of making up histories for words he had plucked from his imagination, he researched the histories of real words. His title, lexicographer, meant "writer of vocabulary." In reality, Tolkien worked as an archaeologist of words. He searched through books from past centuries to find out how and when a word was first used. Then he traced how its meaning changed through time. Few people in England were better qualified for this task than Tolkien. With his knowledge of Anglo-Saxon, Icelandic, Old German, Middle English, and other languages, he could trace words back through the centuries. One OED entry that bore Tolkien's stamp was "walrus."

Later in his life, Tolkien presented a humorous view of dictionary-making in his story *Farmer Giles of Ham*. He advised readers who wondered what a "blunderbuss" was to check with the "four wise clerks of Oxenford." Slyly, Tolkien poked fun at the chief editors of the OED: Craigie, Murray, Bradley, and Onions. A "blunderbuss" is a person who makes stupid mistakes. The word originally described a poorly designed seventeenth-century gun.

Tolkien said that he learned more about words in this period of his life than at any other time. Later, when editors were preparing *The Hobbit* for publication, one editor complained that he could not find a word that

A to Z

Early Greek and Latin dictionaries did not list every word, as dictionaries do today. They included only difficult or rare ones. Historians credit Robert Cawdrey, a teacher, with publishing the first English dictionary in 1604. Entitled *A Table Alphabeticall of Hard Wordes,* it listed three thousand English words. Samuel Johnson and Noah Webster were other famous makers of dictionaries.

Tolkien had used in the dictionary. Tolkien replied, "I wrote the Oxford English Dictionary!" Few tasks in life brought Tolkien more joy than being invited to contribute one final word to the OED in 1970. The editors of that revision asked Tolkien to define "hobbit."

PROFESSOR IN TRAINING

Oxford awarded Tolkien a master's degree in 1919, but that title was honorary only. He received it automatically for residing at the university for five years. In his spare time, Tolkien continued his language invention and his studies of mythology. *Beowulf*, the Anglo-Saxon poem, continued to fascinate him. After his days working on the *New English Dictionary*, Tolkien spent his nights researching northern myths. All the northern languages he had studied—Icelandic, Finnish, Welsh, Anglo-Saxon, Old German— became tools in that investigation.

To earn more money, Tolkien began to tutor undergraduate students. When he was hired for the job, the interviewer asked him an odd question—whether he was married. Tolkien would be tutoring many female undergraduates who were entering the university for the first time. When Tolkien said that he was, the interviewer felt reassured. In those days, people preferred that single men did not tutor single women.

English universities differ from American ones. In England, students attend lectures and meet with tutors for one-on-one instruction. Each week, Tolkien's students each brought him a three-thousand-word essay on a particular subject. Tolkien discussed the ideas in the essay with his student and then connected these concepts to other works of literature.

Because Ronald and Edith had both been raised as orphans, they became very active, caring parents. The family grew to include four children. Although Tolkien could have tutored students on campus, he chose to meet them at his home so he could spend more time with his family.

OPPORTUNITY STRIKES

A great misfortune provided Tolkien with his next important career opportunity. A professor of English at the University of Leeds drowned. The school wanted an Anglo-Saxon specialist to replace Professor F. W. Moorman. Tolkien applied for the position. At age twenty-eight, he was one of the youngest applicants. His knowledge of Old English and his fluency in other languages greatly impressed the staff. They offered him the position of reader in the English language. In England, a reader teaches college students in the same way as a professor does, but has a lower rank.

The family moved to Leeds. Leeds is located halfway between London and Scotland. As a manufacturing city, it had thousands of factories that made many products—everything from boots to bullets, engines to ships.

In the 1920s, when the Tolkiens moved there, the city was very polluted. Soot from coal-fired factories coated everything with grime: clothes, curtains, and even Tolkien's white shirt collars. According to Priscilla and John Tolkien in *The Tolkien Family Album*, their father had to change his shirt collars three times a day. In those days, shirt collars were detachable and could be removed without changing the whole shirt.

One aspect of life in Leeds that Tolkien greatly enjoyed was hearing the distinctive West Yorkshire dialect. He also recognized words distinct to this region. Tolkien found many of them familiar. His favorite professor, Joseph Wright, had come from this area of the country.

After living in peaceful Oxford, Tolkien did not enjoy the huge, dirty city. He also found his students to be much less capable than the ones at Oxford. "Dull stodges" is how Tolkien described them years later in a letter to his son, Christopher. But Tolkien grew to admire these Leeds students. They worked very hard. In that same letter, he told Christopher that he

Leeds, which is located in the Aire valley, has been a transportation hub for England for centuries. Unlike most English cities, it has easy access to both the east and west coasts.

preferred to teach the less bright Leeds students than to work with more intelligent students who did not care as much about their learning.

During his first term at Leeds, Ronald applied for a position in South Africa, where he was born. When the University of Cape Town offered the young professor a position, he felt tempted to accept it. The land of his birth still exerted a strong pull on him. But Edith convinced him that it would be a difficult move because of their growing family.

Tolkien developed the language program at the University of Leeds. He did a tremendous amount of work organizing courses and teaching them. In a letter dated June 27, 1925, he listed the courses he taught there. They included Old English heroic verse, the history of English, various Old and Middle English texts, Old and Middle English philology, introductory Germanic philology, Gothic, Old Icelandic, and Medieval Welsh.

During those years, he also worked hard on research. With the scholar E. V. Gordon, he published his first book, *A Middle English Vocabulary*. This work was not intended for popular reading. It was designed for scholars. Also with Gordon, he worked on a new edition of *Sir Gawain and the*

Color Camelot Green

No one knows who wrote the original version of *Sir Gawain and the Green Knight*. In the poem, the Green Knight barges into a Christmas celebration. He rides a green horse and wears only green. From his huge ax, a strip of green fabric floats. The Green Knight challenges King Arthur to an ax-striking contest.

Green Knight. This work was so successful that it is still used by students today. Tolkien was promoted to a professorship at the University of Leeds in 1924. He became the youngest professor at the university.

Tolkien learned to care for and admire his students. To make language-learning more fun, he developed crossword puzzles. He wrote the clues in Anglo-Saxon. With Gordon, he formed a Viking Club. Faculty members gathered with students to read sagas in Old Icelandic. Some nights, students translated nursery rhymes into Old English. The group even invented original Anglo-Saxon songs. This collection of "old" songs grew. Finally, the group members had enough songs to publish a collection, which they titled *Songs for the Philologists.*

Throughout his career, Tolkien fought to close the gulf that divided the faculty of literature from the faculty of language. He could not understand why they could not work together easily, but Tolkien, too, had prejudices. Although he loved poems and Middle-English texts, he thought that literature should be a subset of language. He wanted to name his department the Department of English Language rather than the Department of English Literature.

During those years of teaching and fulfilling family responsibilities, Tolkien did not forget his invented languages, nor the land called Middle-earth. Most nights, after his children went to bed, he worked on *The Book of Lost Tales.* His oldest sons, John and Michael, were growing older. Soon Tolkien would have an audience for his invented world.

C. S. Lewis was born in Belfast, Ireland, in 1898. For over twenty-five years, he was Tolkien's closest friend.

NINE

Oxford Again

During the summer of 1925, a wonderful position opened at Oxford. W. A. Craigie, Tolkien's former tutor and editor of the *New English Dictionary*, resigned. Tolkien applied for his position, but without much hope. Professorships at Oxford were rare. Competition for the job would be fierce.

Earning a professorship at Oxford is considered a high honor. At American universities, many faculty members receive that title, but at Oxford, the opposite holds true. Of thirty members of the English faculty then at Oxford, only three had achieved that rank. Tolkien held two separate professorships during his thirty-four years there. On the other hand, C. S. Lewis, the famous author of the *Chronicles of Narnia*, was never offered one.

Because it was founded more than eight centuries ago, Oxford has many traditions. Until the end of the nineteenth century, none of its faculty could marry. An example of a medieval tradition still practiced in Tolkien's day was the welcoming ceremony. C. S. Lewis, who joined the faculty about the time Tolkien did, described his welcoming ceremony to Magdalen College in a letter to his father written in August of 1925. Lewis had to kneel on a red cushion while the college president addressed him in Latin. *Do fidem*, Lewis replied, pledging his faith. The president pulled Lewis up, saying, "I wish you joy." Afterwards, Lewis shook hands with all of the faculty members. Each repeated the phrase "I wish you joy."

At Oxford the teaching day lasted many hours. The dons were expected to attend chapel at 8 A.M. and then share breakfast together in the Common Room. Student tutorials were held from 9 A.M. to 1 P.M. In the afternoons, the dons gave lectures or did research. Dinner was held at 7:15 P.M. On some nights, students gathered after dinner to read and discuss literature until 11 P.M.

Tolkien did not live in his rooms on campus, as many dons did. To spend more time with his family, he often met students at his home. In an

Express from the North Pole

The first letter from Father Christmas arrived when John was three years old. For twenty years, the Tolkien children—John, Michael, Christopher, and Priscilla—received illustrated letters from the North Pole. Each described a series of humorous accidents, any one of which could have prevented Father Christmas from reaching the Tolkiens' roof that year. Each Christmas, the cast of characters grew, but the North Pole Bear remained a continual favorite.

interview with Shirley Lowe, Priscilla, Tolkien's daughter said, "He took his job as head of the family very seriously and he was always there, at lunch and at tea. We children were allowed to run in and out of his study at any time, so long as he wasn't actually teaching."

Tolkien had to hurry between home and campus several times each day. In those days, dons were expected to wear long, black robes. Tolkien raced around Oxford on a bicycle. His robes sailed in the air behind him. These flying robes gave him a mysterious, almost medieval look.

FOREST SPIRITS VISIT THE UNIVERSITY

John Lawlor, who was a student of both Tolkien and C. S. Lewis, described Professor Tolkien's appearance. In his book *C. S. Lewis: Memories and Reflections*, Lawlor wrote, "Tolkien was unmistakably good-looking—a well-shaped head, delicate hands and feet, and, rarity among donnish heads, well-combed hair." Lawlor also reported that when he first met Tolkien, "my first and abiding impression was of immediate kindness."

A writer for the *Times* of London once called Tolkien "the best and worst talker in Oxford." Best because his knowledge was deep and his enthusiasm extraordinary. Worst because he spoke fast and often mumbled. Occasionally, Tolkien began to lecture while striding down the hallway before entering the lecture hall. The fact that he usually spoke with a pipe jammed into his mouth did not help. In a *New York Times* interview on March 3, 1957, Tolkien himself said, "I am told that I talk in shorthand and then I smudge it."

Nevertheless, C. S. Lewis advised his students to attend Tolkien's lectures. In his essay "Recollections of J. R. R Tolkien," George Sayer, a student of both men, recalled how Lewis recommended the professor. Lewis praised Tolkien. He said he knew languages better than anyone else. Lewis also believed that the professor made brilliant asides. He called Tolkien "an inspired speaker of footnotes." As John and Priscilla Tolkien recalled in *The Tolkien Family Album*, a former student, J. I. M. Stewart, described the sense of wonder that Tolkien brought to a classroom. Stewart said, "He could turn a lecture room into a mead hall, in which he was the bard and we were the feasting, listening guests."

Tolkien lectured about *Beowulf, Sir Gawain and the Green Knight*, the legends of King Arthur, and other works from the northern European world. He shared sagas, runes, and medieval poems. He introduced students to knights, kings, fairies, elves, monsters, giants, and dwarfs. Also detailed were battles, beheadings, quests, the killing of evil monsters, and contests of skill. He told about great feasts with tables overflowing with meat and wine. He described how people traveled on difficult journeys and then struggled to return home again.

BITING COAL BY THE FIRE

Soon after arriving at Oxford, Tolkien decided to form another club. As always, he wanted to share his passion for literature with others. The northern works he found in the Bodleian Library were too good to read silently and alone. They needed to be shared with a group. These medieval legends were composed in a circle of storytellers and listeners. Tolkien wanted to free them from the page and bring them back before an audience.

Tolkien organized a club called "the Coalbiters." He named it that because the attendees—mostly other faculty members—sat so close to the fire that if they wanted to, they could have reached out and grabbed a burning coal. The Coalbiters read and translated Old Icelandic texts. Lewis, who did not know Old Icelandic when he joined, was overjoyed to hear the myths and legends spoken in their original language. Since childhood, he had felt a strong attachment to these stories. He and Tolkien both loved all things northern. This shared interest brought the two men together as friends.

Tolkien continued to teach legends and myths. At the same time, he worked on his own writing. For twenty years, Tolkien had steeped himself in these tales. Finally, his "mythology of England" was beginning to simmer.

FATHER STORYTELLER

In the end it was neither Tolkien's research on languages nor his fascination with the past that pushed him to write fiction. His children inspired him. They asked him each night for another story. Sometimes, the children requested particular characters. They wanted to hear about elves or dwarfs or Gaffer Gamgee. Michael, who shared his father's love of trees and horror when any were cut down, requested a story about magical treelike creatures.

In an interview in *The Sunday Telegraph* in 1973, Michael recalled his father's incredible bedtime stories. Michael said that these stories were "infinitely more exciting and much funnier" than any published children's books of that period. Michael believed the factor that made his father's stories truly exceptional was "that quality of reality, of being inside a story and so being part of it. . . ." The Dutch professor, S. T. R. O. d'Ardenne, recognized this characteristic of Tolkien's stories as well. "You broke the veil, didn't you, and passed through?" she asked in her book about Tolkien's work.

Unfortunately, Tolkien wrote none of these first stories down. However, in 1925, Ronald told one story that he decided to record. On a vacation to the coast, Michael, who was then five years old, lost a favorite toy dog. In the excitement of playing by the sea, he dropped it on the beach. Tolkien and his sons searched for it, but could not find it. Michael felt very sad.

To cheer him up, Tolkien made up a tale about a dog named Rover. A wizard changed Rover into a toy dog named Roverandom. This became the title of the story. Roverandom had many adventures, including meeting a sand-sorcerer. He rode a moon-path up to the moon. Another time, he hitched a ride on a seagull. This story featured many unique characters, including a wizard, a white dragon, a sea serpent, and even the man in the moon. That is how Tolkien changed a child's sadness about losing a favorite toy into a children's fantasy tale.

TEN

On Hobbits
and Fairy Stories

"**M**y stories seem to germinate like a snowflake around a piece of dust," Tolkien once said to journalist Philip Norman, but writing books was never that easy for him. He toiled on *The Hobbit* for about eight years and on *The Lord of the Rings* for twelve. He worked on *The Silmarillion* for more than fifty years!

What exactly is a hobbit? In the dictionary definition Tolkien wrote, he described a hobbit as "one of an imaginary people, a small variety of the human race. . . ." Tolkien reported that they lived in holes. Critics believe that Tolkien transformed the good, honest people of Sarehole into these creatures with furry toes. Others believe that he modeled them after the

This is a still from *The Hobbit*, the 1977 animated feature film, which introduced a whole new generation to the small people of the Shire.

brave soldiers of World War I. Tolkien wrote that he was "a Hobbit (in all but size). . . ." in a letter to author Deborah Webster Rogers.

Tolkien's children remembered first hearing "hobbit" stories in the late 1920s. However, it was not until 1930 that Tolkien wrote down the opening words to *The Hobbit* while he was grading examination papers. Because of the low salaries professors received, Tolkien made extra money by grading examination papers for seventeen years. When he turned one over and found a blank page, the words flowed out.

Tolkien insisted that he didn't really write his stories, but merely typed them onto the page. As he pecked away at his typewriter, he was describing a world that already existed. As a deeply religious man, he believed that only God could create. He considered himself not a writer, but a "sub-creator."

Only Tolkien could have written his fantasy novels. No one else knew more about myths, runes, and legends than he did. No other writer had such a broad command of so many languages. As a professor who taught the history of English, he understood what made languages tick better than anyone. He understood how to use roots to make up new words. Few other modern writers felt as drawn as Tolkien did to the distant past.

Tolkien transformed himself as an author. He went from writing a scholarly book called *A Middle English Vocabulary* to writing several of the best novels of the twentieth century. Four children inspired that great change. Their names were John, Michael, Christopher, and Priscilla. Tolkien dedicated *The Hobbit: Or There and Back Again* to his children.

According to the author, these novels began with the names. Tolkien chose interesting names that energized his imagination. A few of these names include Bilbo, Smaug, Lugdush, and Valandur. Bilbo received his name because he had a long, thin sword that was made in Bilbao, Spain. In *The Hobbit*, the character Bilbo also carries such a sword.

Warning: Wrong Century

If Tolkien had written historical fiction instead of fantasy, critics could have accused him of using anachronisms in his writing. An ananchronism (from the Greek, meaning "against time") consists of something that occurs at the wrong historical time. For instance, Tolkien wrote about daily mail delivery, which did not begin in England until the 1800s. Also, tobacco did not arrive in Europe until the 1500s. In both cases, Tolkien included details that were not part of daily English life during the time period about which he wrote.

After making up names (and usually changing them several times), Tolkien added languages. He considered languages to be the most important ingredients in his books. He spent years developing them.

HOBBIT BLOOD

Tolkien typed much of *The Hobbit* in the study of his house on Northmoor Road. He worked on the manuscript in the early hours of the morning. Tolkien shared sections of it with his children as bedtime tales. He also received feedback on it from the members of his latest club, the Inklings.

In a letter written in September of 1967, Tolkien recalled the origin of the Inklings. Originally, an undergraduate had started the club. He wanted it to continue for more than a few seasons. Therefore, he invited several dons to join. By the time Tolkien became a member, the Inklings no

C. S. Lewis (the man wearing the hat) organized many of the Inklings meetings. In one of his books he wrote, that two is far from being the necessary number for friendship. Lewis felt that each additional member of a group drew out new aspects of the others' personalities.

A Famous Pub

The building that housed The Eagle and Child had a long history. During the English Civil War, citizens dropped off supplies there for Charles I's army. They brought cows or grain to feed the army in its fight against the Roundheads. Because many people in the seventeenth century could not read, a sign maker put the local earl's coat of arms on the sign. He painted the image of an eagle and a child.

longer included any college students. It included professors, a lawyer, a historian, a doctor, a retired army officer, and an editor. Although people later rumored that mystery writer Dorothy Sayers had joined, no women were ever included.

C. S. Lewis, Tolkien's fellow professor, described a typical Inkling gathering. In a letter to his brother written in November of 1939, Lewis recorded the "bill of fare" of the latest meeting. It included Tolkien sharing a section from his new hobbit book and a nativity play by Charles Williams. Lewis himself read a chapter of nonfiction on the "Problem of Pain."

On Thursday nights, C. S. Lewis hosted the group in his rooms at Magdalen College. Lewis's brother, Warnie, brewed tea. The author of the Narnia books did not mind if someone dropped ashes onto his rug. Lewis jokingly told them to rub it in. In response, the Inklings called Lewis's rooms "The Midden." In Middle English, *midden* meant dunghill.

In later years, after Lewis accepted a professorship at Cambridge, the Inklings switched their meeting place to a pub called The Eagle and Child. They met there for lunch on Tuesdays. Locals nicknamed this pub The Bird and Baby.

Tolkien and Lewis shared a deep friendship. Although members of the same faculty, they represented warring factions. Lewis belonged to the literature group; Tolkien, the language group. But writing, a love of myths, and eventually Christianity brought them together. Lewis affectionately called Tolkien "Tollers."

One day, each agreed to write a book of fantasy. Lewis suggested that he begin one on space travel, while Tolkien write one on time travel because he could write about the past so well. Tolkien began one that he never finished called *The Lost Road*. Lewis completed *Out of the Silent Planet*, which he eventually published. Soon Lewis began his Narnia books, in which children journey to another world by climbing inside a large wardrobe. Many years later, Tolkien finished *The Lord of the Rings*, which he set in the distant past.

Members of the Inklings brought manuscripts to share at their meetings. Lewis shared his

The Eagle and Child, the popular downtown pub where the Inklings met, is now a famous Oxford tourist attraction.

Narnia books. Tolkien read *The Lord of the Rings*, chapter by chapter. The group did not always praise what Tolkien wrote. Members often offered criticism. In a letter written on February 8, 1967, Tolkien recalled that Lewis often pushed him to write better.

When *The Lord of the Rings* was eventually published, Tolkien acknowledged his debt to his fellow Inklings. Tolkien dedicated the book to his children, and also to "the Inklings, because they have already listened to it with a patience, and indeed with an interest that almost leads me to suspect that they have hobbit-blood in their venerable ancestry."

Without feedback from his friends, Tolkien never would have become the great writer that he became. The Inklings gave Tolkien what every writer needs—an interested audience. When Ronald finally finished the manuscript of *The Lord of the Rings*, he asked Lewis for his opinion of it. Lewis liked it immensely. In a letter written in September of 1965, Tolkien

Tolkien appreciated the emotional support he received from C. S. Lewis regarding his writings.

described Lewis's faith in him. Tolkien said he felt indebted to his friend not for his help or advice, but for his "sheer encouragement."

REPORT FOR A SHILLING

Ronald never looked for a publisher for *The Hobbit*. He wrote the book for his own and his children's entertainment. He never intended it for the world's view. As his children grew older, he worked on it less and less. If C. S. Lewis had not encouraged him, Tolkien never would have finished the manuscript.

As soon as he did, word of the story spread throughout campus. An Oxford graduate told an acquaintance that Tolkien had penned an interesting children's story. This acquaintance, Susan Dagnall, worked for a publisher. She visited Tolkien at home and asked to see the manuscript.

Dagnall worked for George Allen & Unwin, a leading British publisher. Sir Stanley Unwin, its director, had a wise process for selecting children's books. He asked his own children to read them. Sir Stanley's theory was that if one child liked a book very much, others would as well. So

A Dream Machine

Tolkien did most of his own typing until his sons, Michael and Christopher, grew old enough to help him. The author dreamed of having a special typewriter built to order. Tolkien's dream typewriter would offer letters in his own Quenyan script.

Rayner Unwin, age ten, had the opportunity to judge *The Hobbit*'s worth for publication. For his trouble, Sir Stanley paid him one shilling.

Rayner recommended *The Hobbit* very highly. In his book about publishing, *George Allen & Unwin: A Remembrancer,* Rayner included his official report about the book. "Billy Baggins was a hobbit who lived in his hobbit-hole and *never* went for adventures, at last Gandalf the wizard and his dwarves perswaded [sic] him to go. He had a very exciting time fighting goblins and wargs. . . ." Rayner recommended the book for "all children between the ages of 5 and 9." That is how the opinion of a ten-year-old launched Tolkien's publishing career.

This photograph shows the cover from one of many editions of *The Hobbit*. First editions of Tolkien's first book now sell for $65,000. Signed copies are even more valuable.

ELEVEN

Hobbits and Beyond

*T*he *Hobbit* was published in September of 1937. By Christmas, all fifteen hundred copies had sold out. George Allen & Unwin rushed out a new edition. This time, it included Tolkien's illustrations. Soon, enthusiastic hobbit fans, or hobbitomanes as writer Anthony Thwaite dubbed them, began forming. Rayner Unwin read the book again, this time for fun. All told, Rayner read *The Hobbit* eight or nine times as a child.

Sir Stanley Unwin, the publisher, met with Tolkien. He asked for a sequel, or a follow-up book on the same subject. Tolkien promised one. Unfortunately, the publisher would not see *The Lord of the Rings* for seventeen more years. At first, Tolkien offered his *Book of Lost Tales*, which he had renamed *The Silmarillion*.

The manuscript that Sir Stanley's readers saw bore no similarity to any completed novel they had ever seen. First, *The Silmarillion* consisted of both prose and poetry. Second, more than fourteen languages were used. Most of them were invented languages. Third, they could not distinguish a story line or even figure out who was telling the story. No Bilbo Baggins (the main character in *The Hobbit*) led them on a series of adventures. Although the publisher knew that he could sell many copies of a *Hobbit* sequel, they did not believe that this unfinished manuscript could succeed in the marketplace.

FIFTY YEARS IN THE MAKING

Tolkien believed *The Silmarillion* to be his most important book. He started working on it in hospital beds during World War I while recovering from trench fever. During his lifetime, he never completed it.

In his memoir about his publishing company, Rayner Unwin recalled that Tolkien believed his third major book to be "a necklace of jewels that lacked a string." At the time Rayner wondered why Tolkien could not simply sit down and finish it. After Tolkien's death, his son Christopher spent many years gathering and finishing those tales of Middle-earth. It was not until then that Rayner understood what a complex and lengthy task Tolkien had given himself.

In *The Silmarillion*, Tolkien tried to include all that he had learned about myths, legends, poetry, and language. Also included, although he would never admit it, was all that he had learned about suffering from living through two brutal world wars. His Catholicism also influenced *The Silmarillion*, the emphasis of which was on good and evil.

The task Tolkien had given himself was impossible; even harder than the quests made by the hobbits in his book. For one man to create a

Cabbage Lane

Although Tolkien later complained about destructive automobiles, in the 1930s, his family owned two cars. They named the first Old Jo; the second, Jo 2. On a trip to his brother's farm, Tolkien drove into a wall. Tolkien's bad driving inspired *Mr. Bliss*, one of his children's stories. Mr. Bliss smashed into things. He crashed into Day's cabbage cart and Knight's donkey cart, which was piled high with bananas. In real life, Edith dreaded taking a car trip with her husband.

mythology for a modern country was impossible. Still, Tolkien pressed on with his life's work.

A GAGGLE OF DWARVES

For a professor of languages, Tolkien had an unusual habit. He often used his own spellings for words. Perhaps his dictionary work had taught him how variable the spelling of words can be. Perhaps his ability to invent languages encouraged him to put his own stamp on what he called his "cradle language" (English). In any case, Tolkien occasionally sent his copy editors to study the dictionary. The most famous case was when he made the plural of "dwarf," "dwarves."

In *The Hobbit* manuscript, Tolkien typed "dwarves" each time he came to more than one of the little creatures. An editor gently reminded him that the plural of "dwarf" was "dwarfs." Tolkien admitted to feeling embarrassed that he, a professor of languages, had used the incorrect word. However, he insisted that "dwarves" be used. In Middle-earth, only "dwarves" existed. No ordinary "dwarfs" were allowed. Today, both "dwarfs" and "dwarves" are accepted spellings.

ANOTHER HOBBIT ADVENTURE

When World War II broke out in 1939, all the Tolkien children were grown except for Priscilla. John, the eldest, had become a Catholic priest. Both Michael and Christopher fought in the war. Christopher, the son who shared Ronald's great love for languages, was stationed in the Royal Air Force (RAF) in South Africa. Ronald had begun his second hobbit story. He shared sections with Christopher by letter. Ronald wrote to his son and described how a new character had entered the world of Middle-earth. Tolkien mentioned these characters appearing as though he had no control over them.

The "New Hobbit"—as the Inklings tagged it—which was eventually to become *The Lord of the Rings*, was darker than the original and more serious. Tolkien still labored over *The Silmarillion* at the same time. Parts of this mythology was added to the new work as well. For both books, Tolkien invented a mix of fantastic beings. Each had a name, a history, and a language.

Tolkien, however, had trouble finishing this new work. In December of 1947, Lewis wrote a friend that "Professor Tolkien's second Hobbit is still unfinished; he works like a coral insect you know!!" Another friend, Robert Murray, recalled in the article "A Tribute to Tolkien," Tolkien's fears about writing. Tolkien said, "I have exposed my heart to be shot at."

Tolkien filled his book with authentic details. He never allowed his heroes to travel without packing food. He once told writer Joan McCluskey that he disliked "those old romances where a knight in full armour sets off an a journey without even a cake in his hand."

These photographs are from Peter Jackson's award-winning film adaptation of *The Fellowship of the Ring* released in 2001. Many different types of Tolkien's creations are brought to life in the film, such as elves (top), hobbits (middle), and orcs (bottom). In Tolkien's fantasy world, elves could live forever, hobbits were small but brave, and orcs were dark, evil creatures.

Some Creatures of Middle-earth

BALROG	**An evil spirit that survived the battles of the First Age.**
DRAGONS	**Also known as "Great Worms," the most ancient creatures.**
DWARVES	**Small, chubby, bearded beings. Love working with tools.**
ELVES	**First to use language. The immortal ones.**
ENTS	**Most ancient of all. "The fathers of the fathers of trees."**
HOBBITS	**Half the size of adult humans. Hairy toes. Eat six meals per day.**
ORCS	**Goblinlike creatures. Spend entire lives in the dark.**
TROLLS	**Cannibals. Noon-day sun turns them into stone forever.**
VALAR	**"Guardians of the World." Helped create Middle-earth.**

WIZARDS, ELVES, AND ADDING MACHINES

By the time Tolkien finished his follow-up to *The Hobbit*, Rayner Unwin had grown up, graduated from Oxford University, studied at Harvard, and completed his military service. He now worked for the publishing company. Rayner drove down from London to pick up the new manuscript.

Sir Stanley was traveling around the world then, so it was Rayner's job to decide if they should publish Tolkien's new manuscript, *The Lord of the Rings.* After calculating estimates with his staff, Rayner concluded that even if the book were successful, the firm would lose one thousand pounds. He sent an airmail letter to his father, who was then visiting Japan. He told his father that the book was very good, and that they should publish it. But they would lose money. Rayner recalled what happened next in his book *George Allen & Unwin: A Remembrancer.* Sir Stanley wrote back, "*If* you believe it is a work of genius, *then* you may lose a thousand pounds."

TWELVE

Birth of a Trilogy

"This book is like lightning from a clear sky." With this sentence, C. S. Lewis hailed the first volume of Tolkien's trilogy, *The Lord of the Rings*. In the same review in an August 1954 issue of *Time & Tide*, Lewis described the book with the adjectives "gorgeous," "eloquent," and "unashamed."

Other critics gave it equally magical reviews. "No fiction I have read in the last five years has given me more joy than *The Fellowship of the Ring*," poet W. H. Auden wrote in the *New York Times Book Review* in October of 1954. "I cannot imagine a more wonderful Christmas present," he added. However, everyone did not praise the trilogy. Some reviewers hated it. Other readers were confused by it. They wondered if it was a book for children, like *The Hobbit*, or if Tolkien intended it for adults. In a review in the 1956 edition of *The Nation*, Edmund Wilson panned the second volume. He called it "juvenile trash."

Rayner Unwin, now Tolkien's editor, had decided that *The Lord of the Rings* was much too large to be printed as one volume. The manuscript came to more than a thousand pages, plus five detailed appendices. All told, it took up more space than Tolstoy's *War and Peace*. In Britain after World War II, paper was scarce and extremely expensive. Rayner decided that it must be printed as a trilogy. Tolkien argued against this. However, once he realized that the publisher could afford it no other way, he agreed. The three volumes came out in 1954 and 1955.

Readers grew impatient with the delay. When volume two ended with the characters in deep trouble, fans could hardly wait for the third volume. To make matters worse, Tolkien delayed publication of the third volume. Sir Stanley Unwin, the publisher, described the fans' reaction in his memoir, *The Truth About a Publisher*. "Never in over fifty years of publishing have I

The Fellowship of the Ring

BEING THE FIRST PART OF
THE LORD OF THE RINGS
BY
J. R. R. TOLKIEN

George Allen & Unwin Ltd
RUSKIN HOUSE MUSEUM STREET LONDON

This is the title page for *The Fellowship of the Ring*. Rayner Unwin, the editor, decided to publish Tolkien's *Lord of the Rings* manuscript as three separate books.

received so many letters from the public—some intensely humorous, more resentful, but all complaining that they could endure the suspense no longer, and complaining of our cruelty in delaying the publication of Volume 3."

A Sampling of the Languages of Middle-earth

BLACK SPEECH Used only by servants during "The Accursed Years."

ELDARIN The languages spoken by the Eldar. Both Quenya and Sindarin were Eldarin languages.

ENTISH Language of the Ents. Many long phrases and plenty of adjectives. The Elves taught them to speak.

MANNISH TONGUES Spoken by men during the First, Second, and Third Ages.

QUENYA Oldest language ever recorded. Spoken by elves, the oldest creatures.

SINDARIN Language of the Grey-elves. Resembles Quenya. Derived from Welsh, Tolkien's favorite language.

Tolkien is surrounded by many books on the history of languages. For many years, Tolkien used a converted garage for his office.

What many readers liked best about *The Lord of the Rings* was Tolkien's invented languages. Tolkien included fourteen of his own languages in this trilogy. An interesting fact about the book is that only the hobbits can hear all the different languages being spoken. We read the hobbits' dialogue in English, even though they are speaking their own tongue, Westron. In these books, Tolkien included only a handful of Westron words in the index.

SEEKING PERFECTION

During the process of publishing the trilogy, Rayner Unwin discovered that his talented author had an unusual problem. Tolkien wanted the perfect book. Not only did he want it, but the gentle professor demanded it.

Before a book gets published, the author receives proofs, or printed pages of the manuscript in the published format, to correct. Each time Tolkien received proofs, he made many corrections. He corrected so many items that he soon reached the point where the publisher charged for the corrections. Even then, Tolkien insisted that more changes were necessary. Nevertheless,

THE RETURN OF THE KING

...roke to a branch added 'voice'; (2) reversing the *certh* indicated opening ...a 'spirant'; (3) placing the branch on both sides of the stem added voice ...nd nasality. These principles were regularly carried out, except in one ...oint. For (archaic) Sindarin a sign for a spirant *m* (or nasal *v*) was ...quired, and since this could best be provided by a reversal of the sign ...or *m*, the reversible No. 6 was given the value *m*, but No. 5 was given ...e value *hw*.

No. 36, the theoretic value of which was *z*, was used, in spelling Sindarin ...r Quenya, for *ss*: cf. Fëanorian 31. No. 39 was used for either *i* or *y* ...onsonant); 34, 35 were used indifferently for *s*; and 38 was used for the ...equent sequence *nd*, though it was not clearly related in shape to ...entals.

In the Table of Values those on the left are, in cases of disagreement, the ...lues of the older *Angerthas*. Those on the right are the values of the ...warvish *Angerthas Moria*. The Dwarves of Moria, as can be seen, ...troduced a number of unsystematic changes in value, as well as certain ...w *cirth*: 37, 40, 41, 53, 55, 56. The dislocation in values was due mainly ...two causes: (1) the alteration in the values of 34, 35, 54 respectively to *h* ...he clear or glottal beginning of a word with an initial vowel that appeared ...Khuzdul), and *s*; (2) the abandonment of the Nos. 14, 16 for which the ...warves substituted 29, 30. The consequent use of 12 for *r*, the invention ...53 for *n* (and its confusion with 22); the use of 17 as *z*, to go with 54 in ...s value *s*, and the consequent use of 36 as *ng* and the new *certh* 37 for *ng* ...ay also be observed. The new 55, 56 were in origin a halved form of 46, ...d were used for vowels like those heard in English *butter*, which were ...equent in Dwarvish and in the Westron. When weak or evanescent they ...ere often reduced to a mere stroke without a stem. This *Angerthas Moria* ...represented in the tomb-inscription.

The Dwarves of Erebor used a further modification of this system, ...own as the mode of Erebor, and exemplified in the Book of Mazarbul. ...s chief characteristics were: the use of 43 as *z*; of 17 as *ks* (*x*); and the ...vention of two new *cirth*, 57, 58, for *ps* and *ts*. They also reintroduced ...16 for the values *j*, *zh*; but used 29, 30 for *g*, *gh*, or as mere variants of ...21. These peculiarities are not included in the table, except for the ...ecial Ereborian *cirth*, 57, 58.

Tolkien's hand-written notes and corrections can be seen in the margins. Tolkien's printing style was very artistic and influenced by his mother, Mabel.

The Original Oxford Myth Maker

Eight centuries before Tolkien created his Middle-earth books, another Oxford resident recorded tales of an invented time. Geoffrey of Monmouth wrote the Arthurian tales about King Arthur and his knights. Even though Geoffrey invented most of his facts, he published it as though it were a real history. Early British residents prized this work. They loved having their own heroes to compare with those of the Greeks and Romans.

Tolkien felt sympathy for the editors and printers. When he changed paragraphs late in the process, he diligently counted up each word. His changes took up the exact amount of space as the earlier sections that he had replaced. His goal was to make his changes as seamless as possible.

Tolkien's corrections did not stop at publication. After *The Hobbit* arrived in bookstores, he paid his son, Christopher, two pennies for each mistake that he found. After finishing *The Lord of The Rings* trilogy, Tolkien went back and made more changes to *The Hobbit* so that even minor details in all four books agreed.

WIZARD FATHER

In an essay written after Tolkien's death, a former student, S. T. R. O. d'Ardenne, said that what she remembered most about Tolkien was his great love for his family. He often wrote to her about his concern for "his children's health, their comfort, their future; how best he could help them to succeed in life, and how to make their lives as perfect as possible."

All of the Tolkien children remembered their father as an extraordinary parent. After his father died, Michael wrote in the Sunday *Telegraph*, "I, together with my two brothers and my sister, have not only lost a father who retained a close interest in every detail of our lives . . . but a friend of half a century's standing, for he possessed the rare talent of combining fatherhood and friendship."

When he entered the army, Michael also gave the best one-word summary of his father's work. As he filled out form after form, Michael came to question about his father's profession. Michael filled in the word "wizard."

BOOK OF JEWELS

In Tolkien's invented language Quenya, the word *Silmarilli* means jewels—not any jewels, but the most beautiful ones ever created. Only three of

This map of Middle-earth created for *The Lord of the Rings* movie trilogy in 2001. Tolkien sketched his own map of Middle-earth while he was writing *The Hobbit*. Tolkien wanted his maps to resemble real historical documents.

these *Silmarilli* existed. Feanor, a High-Elven, had crafted these jewels. The tales of *The Silmarillion* could be compared to these jewels. Tolkien mined his lifelong study of languages and myths to create them. Then he polished them and polished them to make them as beautiful and authentic as possible.

Tolkien's great regret was that he did not finish *The Silmarillion*. Even though his publisher begged for a sequel to *The Lord of the Rings*, Tolkien could not be hurried. Tolkien struggled to compose a complete mythology. To make the task more difficult, he had to bring to life all the creatures that peopled Middle-earth. He also needed to give creatures a language, a history, a past. He then needed to describe the geographic features of Middle-earth—its mountains and caves, its rivers and valleys.

Some critics think that Tolkien never finished *The Silmarillion* because he could not make all of the thousands and thousands of details agree. Once he published *The Hobbit* and *The Lord of the Rings*, his myths became grounded in the physical world. They could no longer fly freely in any direction. Tolkien's published books created a static world that he could no longer change easily.

Elven Time

In Middle-earth, elves used "The Reckoning of Rivendall" as their calendar. Days lasted from sunset to sunset. Elves liked to count time in units of six or twelve. For instance, they had six seasons: spring, summer, autumn, fading, winter, stirring. Instead of years, they counted time in *yeni*, which were equal to 144 years.

TO BE CONTINUED

Toward the end of his life, Tolkien realized that he would never complete his mythology. The task was immense. His son, Christopher, agreed to finish the work. Christopher had also studied philology at Oxford. He followed his father's path and became an Oxford don.

Other than Ronald himself, Christopher knew and understood the world of Middle-earth better than anyone. Tolkien was pleased. Someone extremely capable would complete his life's work. More importantly, he could trust his imaginary Middle-earth and his invented languages to someone very close to his heart. Many more of Tolkien's books were published after his death than during his lifetime with Christopher acting as editor.

THIRTEEN

The Shire Lives On

In the 1960s, hobbitmania spread like wildfire across North America. Hobbit societies formed. *Lord of the Rings* graffiti appeared on subway walls. People wore buttons that announced "Frodo Lives," "Gandalf for President," and "Support Your Local Hobbit." Book bags displayed banners that said "Reading Tolkien Can Be Hobbit Forming." Tolkien's novels flew off bookstore shelves. One parent remarked, "To go to college without Tolkien is like going without sneakers."

Fame did not come immediately. Not until almost a decade after *The Lord of the Rings* was published did Tolkien become an international sensation. By then he was in his late sixties. Enthusiastic letters penned in Elvish arrived in Tolkien's mailbox. Even on the remote island of Borneo, fans gathered to discuss Elvish and Sindarin.

Although Tolkien felt happy that he finally had a large audience for his novels, he hated receiving phone calls from the United States at 3 A.M. He remembered how Warnie Lewis handled the endless phone calls that came after his brother's Narnia books became very popular. Warnie answered the phone "Oxford Sewage Disposal Unit." He repeated the phrase until the unwanted caller hung up.

Another problem developed. In the United States, the company Ace published a pirated, or illegal, edition of *The Hobbit*. Tolkien had to spend precious time and energy to fight to protect his work. Answering hundreds of fan letters also took time away from his writing.

In 1959, Tolkien retired from Oxford. Following tradition, he gave a speech summarizing his years at the university. In his "Valedictory Address," Tolkien humorously described having "sat uneasily on the edge of two chairs." He was referring to the rare honor of having received two professorships at Oxford. He also said that he still considered himself only an amateur in his field. Even though he chose to work only on what he

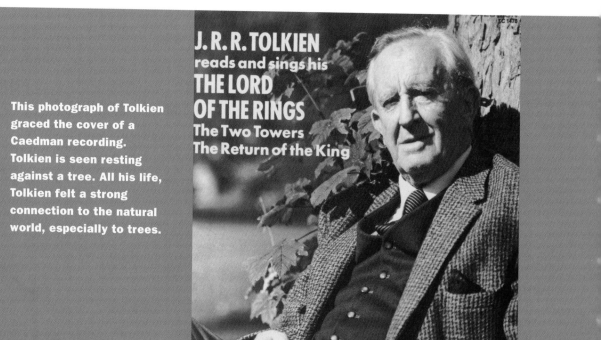

This photograph of Tolkien graced the cover of a Caedman recording. Tolkien is seen resting against a tree. All his life, Tolkien felt a strong connection to the natural world, especially to trees.

himself enjoyed, it also meant "that I have tried to awake *liking*, to communicate delight in those things that I find enjoyable."

The Tolkiens finally had extra money. Edith, whose health had grown poor, wanted to live by the sea. So the Tolkiens left Oxford for Bournemouth. Because Edith suffered from arthritis, they spent many days at the Hotel Miramar, a residential hotel, which lay on a cliff over the English Channel. This was the same Dorset coast that Father Francis had brought Ronald and Hilary to on summer vacations after their mother had died. Tolkien tried to write every day. Often when he was not writing, he often worked on crossword puzzles. Language always remained his passion.

FAREWELL TO LÚTHIEN

Edith Tolkien died in November of 1971. She and Ronald had been married for more than fifty years. Sadness overwhelmed Tolkien. He wrote the following inscription for his wife's headstone:

Edith Mary Tolkien

1889–1971

Lúthien

In *The Silmarillion*, Lúthien was the most beautiful elf. She fell in love with Beren when he called out the word "Tinuviel." It was Lúthien's true name. Lúthien loved Beren very much; so much that she gave up her Elven immortality to join him after he died.

Merton College, Oxford, where Tolkien had taught for many years, offered him an apartment after Edith's death. Ronald returned to Oxford. He had moved to the seaside for Edith's sake, but he always felt more at home at the university. In addition to the apartment, Merton College also provided the famous author with two caretakers. To Tolkien's delight, the married couple spoke Welsh. Tolkien enjoyed greeting them in the language he found to be the most beautiful on earth.

Oxford University presented Tolkien with an honorary doctorate in philosophy in 1972. He particularly enjoyed the fact that he was awarded the degree for his work in philology, not for his novels. A year later, the University of Edinburgh awarded Tolkien another doctorate.

BILBO MOURNS

Tolkien died on September 2, 1973. The British newspaper, *The Daily Telegraph*, remembered him through the eyes of a favorite character. The obituary began: "Bilbo found a scrap of black twist and tied it round his arm. The little hobbit wept bitterly. Somewhere in the world of fantasy that J. R. R. Tolkien created, this is happening at the news of his death." His son John led the funeral mass.

Tolkien so loved his pipe that he added a love of tobacco in the characters of his hobbits.

Later, his children added another inscription to the gravestone in Wolvercote Cemetery:

John Ronald Reuel Tolkien

Beren

1892–1973

Beren and Lúthien were together again.

One memorial that Tolkien would have especially liked occurred on the hundredth anniversary of his birth. The Tolkien Society and the Mythopoeic Society planted two trees on Oxford's campus in Tolkien's honor. They named them Telperion and Laurelin after a pair of trees in *The Silmarillion*. In Tolkien's work, the "Two Trees of Valinor" were central to the spinning of the tales. Besides their connection to his writing, Tolkien valued trees for their own sake. An ecologist before ecologists were common, Tolkien always celebrated the spirits of living trees.

Tolkien never called himself a fantasy writer. He considered his novels to be fairy stories. In March of 1939, Tolkien gave a famous lecture in

A Queen's Gift

In 1973, Queen Elizabeth awarded Tolkien the CBE. This stands for the Commander of the Most Excellent Order of the British Empire. King George gave the first of these awards in 1917 to recognize great service by British citizens. For the first time common people could receive this high honor. This award meant Tolkien was on the path to knighthood.

Scotland. During the lecture, he said a surprising thing. Tolkien believed that fairy stories should not be written for children, but for adults.

He explained why fairy stories are necessary. Tolkien said that the world needs fairy stories to help people escape the awful conditions that they endure. Perhaps he felt this way because he had experienced so much horror during World War I. When he gave this lecture, another world war was about to begin.

Besides the need to escape evil, poverty, and war, Tolkien said that fairy tales provide readers with something else: joy. He described this joy as "a sudden and miraculous grace." Through his writing, teaching, parenting, research, and language invention, Tolkien brought much grace into the world, a hobbity kind of grace that only he could have provided.

Timeline

1892 Tolkien is born in Bloemfontein, South Africa, on January 3.

1897 England celebrates Queen Victoria's Diamond Jubilee.

1901 Queen Victoria dies. Her son, Edward VII, becomes king of England.

1902 Tolkien receives a Foundation Scholarship to King Edward VI High School for Boys.

1911 Tolkien receives an Exhibition Scholarship to Oxford University.

1914 World War I begins.

1915 Tolkien achieves First Class Honors and receives his B.A. from Exeter College, Oxford University.

Tolkien enlists as an officer with the Lancashire Fusiliers during World War I.

1916 Tolkien marries Edith Bratt on March 22. He travels to France to fight at the Somme.

1917 The Bolshevik Revolution brings Communism to Russia.

1918 Tolkien begins work on the staff of the *New English Dictionary*.

World War I ends on November 11.

1920 Tolkien receives appointment as Reader at the University of Leeds.

1922 Tolkien publishes *A Middle English Vocabulary*.

1924 Tolkien is appointed Professor of English Language at University of Leeds.

1925 Tolkien edits and publishes *Sir Gawain and the Green Knight*. He becomes Professor of Anglo-Saxon at Oxford University.

1929 Worldwide economic depression begins.

1933 Hitler granted dictorial powers in Germany.

1937 *The Hobbit: Or, There and Back Again* is published.

1939 World War II begins.

1945 Tolkien is appointed Merton Professor of English Language and Literature at Oxford University.

World War II ends.

1954–1955 *The Lord of the Rings* is published in three volumes.

1957 Tolkien is awarded the International Fantasy Award for *The Lord of the Rings.*

1971 Tolkien's wife, Edith, dies.

Queen Elizabeth honors Tolkien with the CBE award. He receives honorary doctorate from the University of Oxford.

1973 Tolkien dies in Bournemouth, England, on September 2.

To Find Out More

BOOKS

Becker, Alida, ed. *A Tolkien Treasury: Stories, Poems, and Illustrations Celebrating the Author and His World*. Philadelphia: Courage Books, 2000.

Collins, David R. *J. R. R. Tolkien: Master of Fantasy*. Minneapolis: Lerner Publications Co., 1992.

Fisher, Jude. *The Lord of the Rings: The Fellowship of the Ring: Visual Companion*. Boston: Houghton Mifflin, 2001.

Neimark, Anne E. *Myth Maker: J.R.R. Tolkien*. San Diego, Ca.: Harcourt Brace & Co., 1996.

Tolkien, J. R. R. *The Annotated Hobbit*. Edited by Douglas A. Anderson. Boston: Houghton Mifflin, 2002.

Tolkien, J. R. R. *Letters From Father Christmas*. Boston: Houghton Mifflin, 1999.

Tolkien, J. R. R. *Poems from the Hobbit*. Boston: Houghton Mifflin, 1999.

Tolkien, J. R. R. *Roverandom*. Boston: Houghton Mifflin, 1999.

Sage, Alison. *The Lord of the Rings: The Fellowship of the Ring Photo Guide*. Boston: Mariner Books, 2001.

ORGANIZATIONS AND ONLINE SITES

American Tolkien Society
P.O. Box 7871
Flint, MI 48507

This nonprofit organization is devoted to the study and enjoyment of J. R. R. Tolkien's works and those of his son, Christopher Tolkien.

Elvish Linguistic Fellowship
2509 Ambling Circle
Crofton, MD 21114
http://www.elvish.org

This organization is devoted to the study and use of the languages invented by Tolkien.

The Encyclopedia of Arda
http://www.glyphweb.com/arda

This is an online encyclopedia which provides information about the worlds Tolkien created. The name "Arda" was used by Tolkien's elves to describe their world and everything in it.

Houghton Mifflin, Official Publisher's Site for *The Lord of the Rings*
http://www.houghtonmifflinbooks.com.features/lordoftheringstrilogy/

This site provides a detailed history of Tolkien's major works, as well as information about the history of Middle-earth.

J. R. R. Tolkien Collection
http://www.mu.edu/library/collections/archives/tolkien.html

This site describes the largest collection of Tolkien's manuscripts and papers housed in the United States. It is sponsored by Marquette University in Milwaukee, Wisconsin.

Lord of the Rings
http://www.lordoftherings.net

This site gives comprehensive information on *The Lord of the Rings* films. Sponsored by New Line Cinema, the producer, it features special effects, music, cast lists, costumes, and a listing of the creatures of Middle-earth.

The Mythopoeic Society
http://www.mythsoc.org/

This international organization promotes "the study, discussion, and enjoyment of fantasy and mythic literature," particularly the works of Tolkien and the Inklings group.

National Geographic Society
http://www.nationalgeographic.com/ngbeyond/

This site, sponsored by the renowned National Geographic Society, examines the history behind *The Lord of the Rings*.

Tolkien Net Site
http://www.tolkiennet.com

Sponsored by fans, this site focuses on Tolkien's works about Middle-earth.

The Tolkien Society
http://www.tolkiensociety.org

This site, sponsored by The Tolkien Society, is dedicated to promoting the literary works of J. R. R. Tolkien, especially, *The Lord of the Rings*.

A Note on Sources

To research this book, I visited the Tolkien Archives at Marquette University in Milwaukee, Wisconsin. Besides its extensive papers, it houses the original manuscript of *The Lord of the Rings*. I also did research at the Marion E. Wade Center in Wheaton, Illinois, which stores the work of seven Christian writers, including Tolkien. One exciting part of visiting the Wade Center was seeing Tolkien's original writing desk, which is housed there.

Tolkien's own writings proved invaluable—not only his novels, but also his essays and especially his letters. Humphrey Carpenter's authorized biography also shed much light on Tolkien's life. Books by Stanley and Rayner Unwin documented Tolkien's publishing history. *A Tolkien Treasury* provided background on the author's life and work.

For a sense of what life was like in England in the early 1900s, I found several books of early Birmingham photographs: *How Does Your Birmingham Grow?* and *Victorian and Edwardian Birmingham from Old Photographs*. Kerry York from King Edward's School in Birmingham, England, gave me helpful information about Tolkien's student days there.

To trace the connections between Tolkien and C. S. Lewis, books and letters written by Lewis were important. A. N. Wilson's biography and John Lawlor's *C. S. Lewis: Memories and Reflection* were also helpful.

I consulted many published interviews and articles about Tolkien, including "Tolkien on Tolkien," *Diplomat*, October 1966; "Tolkien Talking," *Sunday Times*, November 27, 1966; "J.R.R. Tolkien Talks About the Discovery of Middle-earth, the Origins of Elvish" by Richard Plotz, *Seventeen*, January 1967; "J.R.R. Tolkien—the Wizard Father" by Michael Tolkien, *Sunday Telegraph*, September 7, 1973; "The Prevalence of Hobbits" by Philip Norman, *Sunday Times*, January 15, 1967; and "The Man Who Understands Hobbits" by Charlotte and Denis Plimmer, *Daily Telegraph Magazine*, March 22, 1968.

—Doris Lynch

Index

About the Author

Doris Lynch earned a master's degree in creative writing from San Francisco State University, and a master's degree in libraries and information studies from the University of California, Berkeley. She has won two individual artist grants from the Indiana Arts Commission: one in fiction and one in poetry. She works as a reference and collection development librarian and orders all the fantasy and science-fiction books for her county library.